READING
SCRIPTURE
CANONICALLY

T0339040

READING SCRIPTURE CANONICALLY

Theological Instincts
for Old Testament Interpretation

MARK S. GIGNILLIAT

Ⓑ
Baker Academic
a division of Baker Publishing Group
Grand Rapids, Michigan

© 2019 by Mark S. Gignilliat

Published by Baker Academic
a division of Baker Publishing Group
PO Box 6287, Grand Rapids, MI 49516-6287
www.bakeracademic.com

Printed in the United States of America

All rights reserved. No part of this publication may be reproduced, stored in a retrieval system, or transmitted in any form or by any means—for example, electronic, photocopy, recording—without the prior written permission of the publisher. The only exception is brief quotations in printed reviews.

Library of Congress Cataloging-in-Publication Data
Names: Gignilliat, Mark S., author.
Title: Reading Scripture canonically : theological instincts for Old Testament
    interpretation / Mark S. Gignilliat.
Description: Grand Rapids : Baker Publishing Group, 2019. | Includes index.
Identifiers: LCCN 2018043173 | ISBN 9780801049118 (pbk. : alk. paper)
Subjects: LCSH: Bible—Canonical criticism. | Bible—Criticism, interpretation, etc. |
    Bible. Old Testament—Hermeneutics.
Classification: LCC BS521.8 .G54 2019 | DDC 221.601—dc23
LC record available at https://lccn.loc.gov/2018043173

ISBN 978-1-5409-6206-5 (casebound)

Unless otherwise indicated, Scripture quotations are from The Holy Bible, English Standard Version® (ESV®), copyright © 2001 by Crossway, a publishing ministry of Good News Publishers. Used by permission. All rights reserved. ESV Text Edition: 2016

Scripture quotations labeled NIV are from the Holy Bible, New International Version®. NIV®. Copyright © 1973, 1978, 1984, 2011 by Biblica, Inc.™ Used by permission of Zondervan. All rights reserved worldwide. www.zondervan.com. The "NIV" and "New International Version" are trademarks registered in the United States Patent and Trademark Office by Biblica, Inc.™

Scripture quotations labeled NRSV are from the New Revised Standard Version of the Bible, copyright © 1989 National Council of the Churches of Christ in the United States of America. Used by permission. All rights reserved.

19 20 21 22 23 24 25   7 6 5 4 3 2 1

In keeping with biblical principles of creation stewardship, Baker Publishing Group advocates the responsible use of our natural resources. As a member of the Green Press Initiative, our company uses recycled paper when possible. The text paper of this book is composed in part of post-consumer waste.

For my students,
in prayerful hope
for a life of continued learning
and devotion

The Bible and its principal Subject
are endlessly fascinating.

CONTENTS

ACKNOWLEDGMENTS

I haven't written many books, but certain features of my acknowledgments appear in every one of them. I thank Chris Seitz, my *Doktorvater*, for modeling the combustive effects of a fertile mind conjoined with a deep knowledge of the theological disciplines, particularly his own field. Don Collett offered constructive insights to several chapters. His friendship and theological mind are gifts I value.

I thank my dean, Timothy George, and Beeson Divinity School's associate dean, Grant Taylor, for their support and encouragement to think and write. My colleagues at Beeson are as collegial and amiable as any professor could hope for. I thank especially Ken Mathews, a colleague whose friendship and wisdom I cherish. I also make especial mention of Lyle Dorsett, who retired last year after decades of faithful teaching in various institutions. I want to honor these two esteemed colleagues for their contributions to our learning community and Christ's church. I am grateful to my student James Henderson for reading a draft of this book. James offered helpful reflections from a student perspective and provided his own substantive input.

Stephen Chapman offered valuable feedback and criticism on a prepublished version of this book. I didn't follow Stephen at every turn, but I remain grateful to him for helping me clarify my thought and writing. Colleagues in the field who provide friendship and candor are gifts. Jim Kinney is an able editor and sagacious critic. He continually pressed me to clarify my audience and trim the rhetorical fat from this volume. The book is better for his critical role in its production. My thanks go out to Jim and the publishing team at Baker Academic. Though it goes without saying, any residual problems in the book are my own.

As always, Naomi and my children are gracious presences in every aspect of my life, including this one. Naomi took the time to read this book and offered invaluable feedback. I remain grateful for her encouragement and commitment to me and our family. I'll admit to feeling disjointed at times between my life as a husband and father and as a teacher/writer. The latter seems light years away when I'm sending kids to home plate while coaching little league. Yet I'm so grateful that God in his providence has combined all these facets of my existence into some kind of symphonic harmony. To God be praise.

Holy Week 2018

INTRODUCTION

I tell my students about an early preaching experience of mine. I was young, in my early twenties. I had taken several years of Greek and emerged from my undergraduate experience with misplaced confidence in my ability to teach and preach the Scriptures. Then my number was called for a preaching engagement. I was ready. I had done it before. Nothing new. With Greek text and commentaries spread around me, I entered the fray as I prepared a sermon series on Hebrews 11. What I wasn't prepared for was the small crisis awaiting me. As I studied, parsed verbs, and explored lexical threads, I realized that the sermons I was writing were primarily descriptive in nature. I was talking *about* Hebrews 11, providing lexical information on "faith," and offering background material on various intertextual traditions. In effect, my sermons were learned (I tried) talks on Hebrews 11. They were not sermons crafted for the sake of an encounter with the living God. I felt stuck.

I'm overstating the narrative a bit, I'm sure. Even my younger self wanted sermons that were truly sermons and not lectures. But I do remember feeling troubled. I felt like I was struggling to put on a blazer that didn't fit right. Something was off. It was the living character of the biblical texts that escaped me. Or at the very least, I struggled to lean into this lived dynamic, the fuzzy line where teaching or description yields to preaching, theologizing, and arrestment. Of course, such an effect remains within the provenance of the Holy Spirit's teaching office. Yet the posture, expectations, and (dreaded word) "methods" that one brings to Holy Scripture will either serve or obstruct Scripture's reason for existence.

I am writing this book with my younger self in mind. I'm talking to him and students of all types who have some working knowledge of the historical-grammatical or historical-critical study of Scripture.[1] I too had some exegetical tools at my disposal, and the target audience of this book is students, broadly conceived, who are not completely new to the scene of biblical studies. Yet, perhaps like me, they feel stuck. They are either searching for or in need of theological and hermeneutical instincts that will help them read and engage Holy Scripture as a living witness.

This book is not a be-all or end-all for this purpose. In fact, my primary, if not sole, focus is on reading the Old Testament. (As an aside: I remain on an exorcist's quest to stamp out Marcion's pestering presence in Christ's church: Marcion, be gone!)[2] Christian readers do well to remember that the New Testament never existed, nor does it have an existence, apart from its relation to the Old Testament.[3] The New Testament authors and early church theologians read the Old Testament as a Christian witness. This kind of reading instinct and strategy has always been with the church. Without much effort one could even argue that the New

---

1. Here I'm thinking of standard works of hermeneutical introduction, such as Douglas Stuart, *Old Testament Exegesis: A Handbook for Students and Pastors*, 4th ed. (Louisville: Westminster John Knox, 2009); Odil Hannes Steck, *Old Testament Exegesis: A Guide to the Methodology*, trans. J. D. Nogalski, 2nd ed. (Atlanta: SBL Press, 1998); William W. Klein, Craig L. Blomberg, and Robert L. Hubbard Jr., *Introduction to Biblical Interpretation*, rev. ed. (Nashville: Nelson, 2004).

2. See a cobelligerent in this quest, Brent A. Strawn, *The Old Testament Is Dying: A Diagnosis and Recommended Treatment* (Grand Rapids: Baker Academic, 2017).

3. In technical theological language, and borrowing from the categories of Christology, the New Testament is *anhypostatic* apart from its relation to the Old Testament.

Testament and trinitarian legacy of the early church would not exist without that interpretive impulse. All of this is to say that the scope of this book, with its focus on the Old Testament, is limited from a Christian canonical standpoint. Nevertheless the Old Testament is fertile soil for working out these Christian reading practices. Theological categories and instincts are requisite for engaging the Old Testament's theological subject matter. So this book should equip readers with a theological grammar and a set of interpretive instincts to aid in their reading of Scripture as an enduring canonical witness.

The book falls into two separate parts. I did not plan this structure at the outset, but in time it became both apparent and appropriate. The first part deals with the material character of the Old Testament. What is the Old Testament? How does its place in the Christian Bible impact our reading of it? What theological commitments are necessary as a first step to faithful reading? These questions and more like them center on the following canonical concerns: What is the significance of Scripture's final form? How is textual intentionality best understood from a canonical/scriptural perspective? This first section concludes with a chapter on textual criticism. Admittedly, the air can become thin when delving into text-critical matters, but textual criticism should not be devalued, because it seeks to establish the scriptural text at its most basic level. Theological categories are necessary for this kind of work as well.

The second part of the book focuses on the Trinity as the Old Testament's essential principle—or better, reality. Does the triune character of God flow from the Old Testament's own internal logic and claims, or is it simply a later Christian imposition on the ancient text in Hebrew or Greek form? And if God is triune, what are the interpretive implications for reading the Old Testament, even when readers recognize that the Old Testament came to be before the full outworking of trinitarian dogma in time? These are big questions whose answers change the interpretive game from beginning to end. To put a focus on this book as a whole, the following question drives the project from beginning to end: *How and why should we read the material of Scripture—words, sentences, paragraphs, books, and so forth—in conjunction with Scripture's theological subject matter?*

As a personal word, I have been intrigued and vexed by this question for some time and will continue to pursue it in various ways. This book is an offering to those who have similar pressing concerns and who, like me, are just somewhere along the way toward answering them. Given the magnitude of the question's subject matter, final formulations will always be around the next bend in the road. Heaping spoonfuls of humility and modesty are needed at every turn. Nevertheless, I do believe critical and creative inquiry into this book's driving question ranges somewhere near the heart of the church's long-term health and faithful witness. That might sound hyperbolic at first hearing. But I don't believe it is. I offer this book to readers in gospel hope.

ABBREVIATIONS

General and Bibliographic

AD	*anno Domini* (in the year of the Lord)
ad loc.	*ad locum*, at the place discussed
BC	before Christ
cf.	*confer*, compare
chap(s).	chapter(s)
D	Deuteronomist source (of the Pentateuch)
E	Elohist source (of the Pentateuch)
ed.	edited by, edition
e.g.	*exempli gratia*, for example
esp.	especially
ESV	English Standard Version
et al.	*et alii*, and others
etc.	*et cetera*, and so forth, and the rest
i.e.	*id est*, that is
J	Jahwist/Yahwist source (of the Pentateuch)
KJV	King James Version
L	Leningrad Codex (Leningradensis)
lect.	lecture
LXX	Septuagint (Greek Old Testament)
MT	Masoretic Text (of the Hebrew Bible)
NIV	New International Version (2011)
NRSV	New Revised Standard Version
P	Priestly source (of the Pentateuch)
rev.	revised
sg.	singular
SP	Samaritan Pentateuch
trans.	translated by, translation

Old Testament

Gen.	Genesis	Song	Song of Songs
Exod.	Exodus	Isa.	Isaiah
Lev.	Leviticus	Jer.	Jeremiah
Num.	Numbers	Lam.	Lamentations
Deut.	Deuteronomy	Ezek.	Ezekiel
Josh.	Joshua	Dan.	Daniel
Judg.	Judges	Hosea	Hosea
Ruth	Ruth	Joel	Joel
1–2 Sam.	1–2 Samuel	Amos	Amos
1–2 Kings	1–2 Kings	Obad.	Obadiah
1–2 Chron.	1–2 Chronicles	Jon.	Jonah
Ezra	Ezra	Mic.	Micah
Neh.	Nehemiah	Nah.	Nahum
Esther	Esther	Hab.	Habakkuk
Job	Job	Zeph.	Zephaniah
Ps(s).	Psalm(s)	Hag.	Haggai
Prov.	Proverbs	Zech.	Zechariah
Eccles.	Ecclesiastes	Mal.	Malachi

New Testament

Matt.	Matthew	1–2 Thess.	1–2 Thessalonians
Mark	Mark	1–2 Tim.	1–2 Timothy
Luke	Luke	Titus	Titus
John	John	Philem.	Philemon
Acts	Acts	Heb.	Hebrews
Rom.	Romans	James	James
1–2 Cor.	1–2 Corinthians	1–2 Pet.	1–2 Peter
Gal.	Galatians	1–3 John	1–3 John
Eph.	Ephesians	Jude	Jude
Phil.	Philippians	Rev.	Revelation
Col.	Colossians		

Part 1

SCRIPTURE'S MATERIAL FORM

1

Scripture and Canon

This book aims to provide an introduction to canonical reading practices for those with some working knowledge of the basic tools of biblical studies. In this sense, the book functions like a hospitable welcome into a very large house rather than a geological survey brushing away the dirt from every potential lead. As will become more obvious as the book progresses, the canonical approach presented in this book resides within the Christian theological tradition. Without the eyes of faith and an ecclesial context for reading and reception, the instincts presented in this volume may appear foreign.[1] The second part of the book is devoted to the most basic and defining facet of Christianity's theological identity:

1. Such a claim does not intend to downplay the benefits gained from other interpretive approaches or faith settings, most especially Jewish approaches to reading the Hebrew Bible. Rather, the identification of this approach with the Christian interpretive tradition is offered in the hope of enhancing dialogue and identifying theological/ecclesial contexts as necessary and legitimate for biblical reading. Jewish and Christian interpretation may agree on the religious and historical forces at work in the canonical process, attending to it and its religious/theological motivations as an important facet of biblical exegesis. Nevertheless, this book offers a reading strategy in which examining Scripture's material form *and* theological subject matter fuses them together on a single hermeneutical horizon. If and when this hermeneutical fusion happens, it will lead to interpretive differences between faith communities. This is to be expected and welcomed. From the Jewish interpretive angle, see esp. Jon

the triune identity of God and the interpretive implications of naming God in this way. Nevertheless, on the front end of our journey,
the theological character of this reading strategy must be sorted
out as well: How do we define important terms? What theological
commitments are required for faithful hearing of the biblical text?

These theological instincts and commitments are the tail wagging
the dog of the canonical approach. God is not a god of the gaps,
fitted in here or there to make sense of interpretive conundrums.
Rather, a doctrine of God's providence undergirds the entire project, including our grappling with the creaturely/human dimension
of the biblical texts—the material classically offered in standard
Old Testament introductions and hermeneutical textbooks. I often
tell my students, at every level of their training in biblical studies,
that without a robust doctrine of God's providence, their interpretive ship will remain rudderless and lost. Without a Christian
metaphysic of some sort (more of this in the second part of the
book), the approach offered here falls apart and fails to persuade.

To propel us out of the gate, this chapter focuses primarily
on two important front matters. First, what does the appeal to
canon entail theologically? Second, when we speak of Scripture
broadly or of the Old Testament in particular, what is it? Along
Aristotelian lines of reasoning, the object of study determines
our methods of study. If this idea holds water, then identifying
Scripture's "whatness," or Scripture's ontology, is a crucial matter
of first importance. As this chapter will claim, faithful readers
cannot identify Scripture's nature apart from its relation to God's
self-revealing and redemption.

Canon and Scripture: Clarifying Terms

A potential brick wall faces the canonical approach right out of
the gate. What exactly does the appeal to *canon* suggest? What

Levenson, "Teach the Texts in Context," *Harvard Divinity Bulletin* 35, no. 4 (2007):
19–21, https://bulletin.hds.harvard.edu/articles/autumn2007/teach-text-contexts.

positive effect does a term like *canon* have on the hermeneutical approach set out in this volume, when its basic, shared definition is so contested? Scholars are of varying opinions when defining canon. The marked tendency within the secondary literature is to distinguish between canon and *Scripture*. On this account, canon serves a more crystalline, formal, and external role when attending to the character of the Old Testament. Canon, as differentiated from Scripture, relates to the external choice of a religious community regarding what books are deemed in or out of their Holy Writ. Canon connotes list. As such, scholarly investigations of canon are located in the world of religious and social history. Here carefully imagined religious-social projections are weighed against empirical evidence in the hopes of gaining further clarity on the historical and religious forces at work in the canon's coming to be—a target whose clear aim is equally matched by unclear evidence.[2]

To place "canon" and "Scripture" in related but distinct silos runs the risk of distorting the internal pressure made by the biblical documents themselves on the community of faith: Jewish and Christian. This is by no means a denial of the historical and religious forces at work in various phases of Jewish and Christian history, forces that properly recognized which books "sullied the hands" and which did not. Nevertheless, canon as list stresses under its own brittleness and allows marginal questions about particular books (is Esther in or out?) a disproportionate influence on the term's usefulness. According to these terms, *canon* as a concept becomes hostage to our ability to sort out the

2. For example, Timothy H. Lim states, "I will use 'canon' to refer to the list of biblical books." *The Formation of the Jewish Canon*, Anchor Yale Bible Reference Library (New Haven: Yale University Press, 2013), 4. "Authoritative scripture," on the other hand, refers to "the collections of authoritative writings that appear before the appearance of the first lists" (4). On this account, Lim sides with the linguistic/conceptual relegation of "canon" to list, a move associated with the likes of Eugene Ulrich and others. In agreement with Sid Leiman, however, Lim's notion of authoritative scripture before the closing of the canon recognizes the theological forces related to the preservation and associative reading practices of certain texts deemed authoritative, such as the books of Moses, the Prophets, and the Psalms. Leiman simply refers to these books as "canonical," a linguistic move Lim does not follow.

CANON AND SCRIPTURE: Defining these two terms remains contested among biblical scholars. Drawing from the resources of the canonical approach, this chapter maintains that *canon* and *Scripture* resist formal distinction. *Canon* functions as a *broad theological category* where multiple matters pertaining to the compositional and editorial processes of biblical books reside. It is not a term relegated to the conceptual realm of a final list of biblical books.

historical *whence*, *when*, and *who* as it pertains to these kinds of problems. These questions remain the material of continued scholarly research.

Put in different terms, the fuzziness at the painting's edge runs the danger of distracting from the whole picture. Questions such as "Did Jesus have a canon?" are answered by a disproportionate appeal to the blurry margins at the edge of the list. In this vein, some would answer this question negatively because of the historical uncertainty about the closure of the last part of the tripartite canon, the Writings (*Ketuvim*), during Jesus's own time. Precisely at points such as these do the categories of Scripture and canon bleed into one another so that distinguishing them becomes a formal matter whose substantial difference is hard, if not impossible, to sustain.

The model on offer here softens the distinction between Scripture and canon. The latter, in terms borrowed from Brevard Childs, functions as a *cipher* that allows ample room for multiple factors contributing to the writing, shaping, and preservation of the biblical materials.[3] From this standpoint, the appeal to "canon" or "canonical" recognizes a beginning and an ending to the process of writing, expanding, editing, shaping, and preserving biblical books. Rather than relegate the term *canon* to the end of that process alone, as the final moment when a book was deemed in or

3. Brevard S. Childs, *Biblical Theology of the Old and New Testaments: Theological Reflection on the Christian Bible* (Minneapolis: Fortress, 1992), 70.

out among a list of other books deemed in or out, the canonical approach allows for more flexibility. The approach offered here takes into account the entire process leading to final "canonization."[4]

Emphasizing the distinction between canon and Scripture formalizes the former, relegating it to the final stage of a long and complex process. Yet a "canon consciousness" is actually embedded in the literature itself, and it exerted pressure on various religious bodies in the creaturely act of canonization or the forming of set lists. To make matters clear, canon registers its proper theological force when it is understood first as an internal property of the biblical texts and second as an external decision or act.

A Brief Excursus on Defining "Canon"

Stephen Chapman ranks as one of the clearer and abler voices for sorting through the problem of defining Scripture and canon in relation to each other.[5] Chapman's approach can be set in conversation with Eugene Ulrich, who takes a different view.[6] The term and concept of "canon" make no appearance in the Bible, according to Ulrich. Where the word *kanōn* appears in the New Testament, it does not refer to an authoritative collection of books (see 2 Cor. 10:13, 15, 16; Gal. 6:16). "Thus, the term and discussion of it are absent from the Hebrew and Greek Bibles, suggesting that the term is postbiblical," concludes Ulrich.[7] Ulrich finds it odd that the term "canon" is not discussed as a reality in Judaism and nascent Christianity, especially if the concept was important.[8] Furthermore, no entry for the term "canon" is found in the *Dictionary of Biblical*

4. The term "canonization" is reserved for the decision-making process of synagogue or church in recognizing which books are in or out. For a helpful theological account of the relationship between recognition of canonical books and the creaturely processes attendant to this recognition, see John Webster, *Holy Scripture: A Dogmatic Sketch* (Cambridge: Cambridge University Press, 2003), chap. 2.

5. See Stephen B. Chapman, "The Canon Debate: What It Is and Why It Matters," *Journal of Theological Interpretation* 4, no. 2 (2010): 273–94.

6. Eugene Ulrich, "The Notion and Definition of Canon," in *The Canon Debate*, ed. L. M. McDonald and J. A. Sanders (Peabody, MA: Hendrickson, 2002), 23, 21–35.

7. Ulrich, "Notion and Definition of Canon," 23.

8. Ulrich, "Notion and Definition of Canon," 23.

Theology or the theologies of Eichrodt and von Rad (though the latter can be challenged).[9] These noteworthy absences, according to Ulrich, should be taken seriously. However, it appears that Ulrich's linguistic claim confuses the lack of a term's presence with a lack of a term's essential concerns. One could as easily conclude that the Bible makes no claims about the Trinity because of the lexeme's absence in the Bible.

Ulrich makes use of Gerald Sheppard's distinction between "canon 1" and "canon 2."[10] The former relates to the ruled character of authoritative books: *norma normans non normata* (the norming norm, which cannot be normed). The latter promotes the notion of list and by its very nature is closed. For Ulrich, to speak of an open canon is self-defeating because the very term *canon* precludes openness. However, Chapman believes Ulrich's use of Sheppard's categories—canon 1 and canon 2—does not do justice to Sheppard's overarching concerns. Sheppard did not see a strict sequential linearity between canon 1 and canon 2, with the latter understood as a sequential consequence to the former. In fact, according to Chapman, "fixity is a pole rather than a stage," just as Sheppard argues.[11] A hyperattentiveness to canon as fixity runs into problems in light of the historical evidence, because "determining the precise time and circumstances of the absolute fixation of the canon is a matter of crucial importance—except for one thing: it is in fact chimerical."[12] In fairness to Ulrich's argument, he seeks for lexical clarity by appealing to the Christian tradition itself. He is not opposed to the terms "canonical" or "canonical process" when speaking of authoritative Scriptures present before the formalization of various lists (Sheppard's canon 1), but he relegates canon proper to the decision to include or exclude. Ulrich's efforts are for the sake of clarifying the scholarly discussion.

9. See *Dictionary of Biblical Theology*, ed. Xavier Léon-Dufour, 2nd ed. (New York: Seabury, 1973); Walther Eichrodt, *Theology of the Old Testament*, trans. J. A. Baker, 2 vols., Old Testament Library (Philadelphia: Westminster, 1961); Gerhard von Rad, *Old Testament Theology*, trans. D. M. G. Stalker (San Francisco: Harper & Row, 1965).

10. See Gerald Sheppard, "Canonical Criticism," in *Anchor Bible Dictionary*, ed. D. N. Freedman (New York: Doubleday, 1992), 1:864–65.

11. Stephen Chapman, "Second Temple Jewish Hermeneutics: How Canon Is Not an Anachronism," in *Invention, Rewriting, Usurpation: Discursive Fights over Religious Traditions in Antiquity*, ed. J. Ulrich, A.-C. Jacobsen, and D. Brakke, Early Christianity in the Context of Antiquity 11 (Frankfurt: Peter Lang, 2012), 284.

12. Chapman, "Second Temple Jewish Hermeneutics," 285.

Childs, on the other hand, would simply call Sheppard's canon 2 *canonization*, while situating more closely the relation of canon 1 to canon 2. In other terms, canon 1 is the precedent reality of canon 2, though with Chapman we do well to remember that fixity is itself a pole rather than a definitive stage. Canon 1 and canon 2 relate to each other materially: one does not exist without the other.

The Significance of Scripture's "Whatness"

The Christian church has never operated without a canon.[13] The church, along with the synagogue, is an institution of the book. Words, sentences, and larger discourse units are of consequence in the church's continued efforts to name, worship, and follow after God. Because this literary dynamic is at the heart of the church's identity, the language of the Christian Scriptures matters, even with its varied forms of human discourse, such as law, poetry, narrative, and didactic expression. While the Bible is human in its source from beginning to end, it resists easy reduction to its human sources alone. God has spoken (*Deus dixit*) and is speaking.[14] The exegetical wrestling with the polyphonic voice of Holy Scripture means coming to terms with God's direct address to his church. Later chapters will explore the hermeneutical implications of Scripture as divine address.

While the human and institutional agents attached to the writing, editing, and preserving of the biblical books should never be diminished, Christians around the world today and from the church's inception dive headlong into the Scriptures for the sake of hearing the word of God.[15] The liturgical conclusion to the

13. Hans von Campenhausen, *The Formation of the Christian Bible* (Philadelphia: Fortress, 1977). Thorny historical questions about the finalization of the New Testament canon often obscure the more rudimentary insight of the Hebrew Scripture's properly basic and canonical role in the apostolic and early church periods.

14. See John Webster's deft handling of the dogmatic relationship between the creaturely character of Scripture and its divine source in *Holy Scripture*.

15. In a public lecture titled "Religion and Literature," T. S. Eliot fulminates against those who reduce religious literature, in particular the Authorized Version

> **CANON AND SCRIPTURE'S ONTOLOGY:** Locating the canon of Scrip-
> ture theologically in God's divine economy of revelation and redemption
> provides a proper appreciation for the canon's nature and role. While God
> and Scripture are differentiated from one another, the latter is a "fitting"
> means by which God determines to reveal himself.

public reading of Scripture uses the present tense for a reason:
"This *is* the word of the Lord." As this book hopes to demonstrate,
the confession of faith regarding Scripture's nature (or ontology,
"what it is") impinges on the interpretive approach taken. In other
words, the subject matter being studied shapes the interpretive
methods used to understand it.

Scripture and God: Differentiated yet Fitting

A classical stream of Protestant thought identified Scripture as
the cognitive principle of theology (*principium cognoscendi
theologiae*). God, according to this stream of thought, is the
essential or ontological principle of theology (*principium es-
sendi theologiae*).[16] Put differently, God is the substantial object

---

of the Bible, to its "literary" merit. Such a reduction is an abuse; it is parasitic if not
pestering. The Authorized Version's literary influence on the English language, muses
Eliot, is not due to its consideration as literature. Rather, its influence stems from its
reception as God's Word. Eliot claims, "Those who talk of the Bible as a 'monument
of English prose' are merely admiring it as a monument over the grave of Christianity." *Selected Prose of T. S. Eliot*, ed. F. Kermode (New York: Harcourt, 1975),
98. Eliot predates "literary criticism" or the rise of literary approaches associated
with figures such as Robert Alter. So his learned rant cannot be read as targeting
"literary approaches" per se. Rather, his criticisms are aimed at a secular sensibility
that values, say, the Authorized Version solely in terms of its literary merit or its signal
position in providing linguistic continuity for the English language. The Authorized
Version's enduring viability, in Eliot's estimation, has little to do with such linguistic
or cultural concerns.

16. Richard A. Muller, *Post-Reformation Reformed Dogmatics: The Rise and
Development of Reformed Orthodoxy, ca. 1520 to ca. 1725*, vol. 2, *Holy Scripture:
The Cognitive Foundation of Theology*, 2nd ed. (Grand Rapids: Baker Academic,
2003), 96, chap. 3.

of Christian theological inquiry. With God as the essential principle and goal of Christian theology, Holy Scripture provides the primary location and material for the intellectual/rational engagement with God: no Scripture, no full apprehension of God.[17] For those predisposed against or unfamiliar with Protestant scholastic modes of theological speech, these categories admittedly run the risk of speculative abstractions. But such risks may be avoided when these somewhat cold categories are seen within God's self-determination to be a God in fellowship with humanity. On this account, Scripture is the loving gift of God to his people so they may continually seek him and order their lives toward him, while resting in the confidence that God has not left our desire to know him within the realm of human self-achievement.[18]

By an act of theological retrieval, John Webster makes use of these Protestant scholastic categories by plotting out the relationship between the cognitive and ontological principles of Holy Scripture.[19] They are related to each other such that to have the one demands the other. The ontological principle, or the truth that God is and he speaks, grounds the cognitive principle as it relates to Holy Scripture. As Webster puts the matter, "Holy Scripture is a function of God."[20] Therefore, Holy Scripture's canonical role as the normative guide for Christian thought and life derives its authority from the loving rule of God. Its textual character remains a dynamic means of continued divine self-disclosure. It is not a static "textual deposit."[21]

17. In theological terms, ontology and economy, though distinct matters, must be kept together. There is no access to the theological reality and forces that gave rise to Scripture apart from the providential economy that produced them.

18. For a recent defense of masculine predicates of the divine, see Sarah Coakley, *God, Sexuality, and the Self: An Essay "On the Trinity"* (Cambridge: Cambridge University Press, 2013).

19. John Webster, *The Domain of the Word: Scripture and Theological Reason* (London: T&T Clark, 2012), 128–29.

20. Webster, *Domain of the Word*, 129.

21. Webster, *Domain of the Word*, 129. The Reformational conjoining of Word and Spirit is another way of addressing the same issue.

Webster's insights into the character of Christian Scripture and its subject matter elicit continued reflection. The following claim is no exception:

> Christian theological reason is not an indeterminate intellectual activ-
> ity, reason in search of an object, but reason to which an approach
> has already been made with unassailable might, to which an object
> has been given. This object represents itself in textual form. The form
> does not exhaust its object—how could a mere text fathom the untold
> depths of God's life? But the form is fitting, and through it theology
> does encounter the divine summons; and so theology is not a free
> science, but bound to (and therefore liberated by) the one in whose
> company it finds itself placed.[22]

A few concluding reflections are worth parsing out from this theologically pregnant passage. The object of inquiry (rational/cerebral) and worship (ascetic/whole person) presses itself on the inquirer/worshiper. Part and parcel of this pressing is the gracious provision of a means to the object of inquiry—namely, Holy Scripture. God as object and Scripture as approach are determinate within the redemptive economy for how God orders the goal and means of our theological pursuits. Still, God and Scripture refuse coequal status in their relationship. In other words, God cannot be exhausted by Scripture's textual form: *finitum non capax infinitum* (the finite is not capable of the infinite). At the same time, "The form is fitting."[23] As a "fitting form," Scripture functions as a witness to God's triune self-disclosure. It does so because God, in his gracious movement toward humanity, determines it to be so. The arguments for Scripture's "fittingness" rest finally on this theological confes-

22. Webster, *Domain of the Word*, 129.
23. On analogy, a similar claim is made regarding the relationship between the persons of the Godhead in their eternal procession and their temporal mission. The particular role of the *personae* of the Godhead in the temporal mission is "fitting" with their particular relation in the eternal processions. See Giles Emery, *The Trinitarian Theology of Saint Thomas Aquinas*, trans. F. A. Murphy (Oxford: Oxford University Press, 2007), 413–19, chap. 15.

> **CANON AS RICH AND FERTILE SOIL:** The internal pressure of the biblical documents leading toward canonization identifies these texts as a means of continued divine self-disclosure. Given the stability and diversity of the Old Testament's content, fresh modes of inquiry and strategies for intensive/cross-associative reading remain a promising field of study for Christian theology.

sion and cannot be sustained by modes of reasoning external to theo-logic.[24]

The differentiated-though-fitting relationship between God and Scripture demands the church's continued giving of itself to the exegesis of Holy Scripture. Because Scripture is *not* God, while at the same time remaining a sanctified means for apprehension *of* God, it follows necessarily that the exegesis of Holy Scripture continues as a never-ceasing activity of Christ's church. This self-giving to the continued reading and hearing of Holy Scripture takes place in recognition of God's dynamic interaction with the church of yesteryear, today, and the future, opening avenues of dialogue with interpreters past and present. This understanding of the canon represses any notion that the exegesis of Holy Scripture has been or ever will be superfluous. The canon's subject matter simply will not allow it.

The Richness and Flexibility of the Old Testament's Material Form

Webster's fine account of the matter may be supplemented by appeal to the flexibility of the Old Testament's own canonical form (more will be said of this in the coming pages). Since God is the subject matter of Scripture, it goes without saying that its

24. See Reinhard Hütter, *Suffering Divine Things: Theology as Church Practice* (Grand Rapids: Eerdmans, 1997), 138–39.

textual form cannot exhaust the subject matter. In part, the diversity of voices within Scripture originates in the richness of its main character and point of interest: God. At the same time, the material form of Scripture itself resists exhaustive treatment, and this despite the enormous amounts of interpretive work given to it over the centuries.[25] Scripture's subject matter is infinite, yet its material form is finite. Nevertheless, the material form of Scripture, finite as it is, is a flower whose budding never ceases in its faithful reception and reading.

Anyone broadly familiar with academic publishing today might find the preceding statement teetering toward the hyperbolic. Do we really need another commentary on Isaiah? The question is fair enough, though I might retort offhandedly, "Yes, we could use another commentary on Isaiah." But the simple point registered here is that the historically conditioned material of the Old Testament has been shaped into larger canonical units, with the intention of cross-associative reading for the sake of continued reflection and actualization. Put simply, the potential for a deeper appreciation of the textual dimension of Holy Scripture remains, despite the voluminous work already given to it. Childs clarifies,

> The canonical process involved the shaping of the tradition not only into independent books, but also into larger canonical units, such as the Torah, Prophets and Writings. For example, law was seen from the perspective of wisdom; psalmody and prophecy were interrelated; and Israel's narrative traditions were sapientialized (cf. Sheppard). The canonical process thus built in a dimension of flexibility which encourages constantly fresh ways of actualizing the material.[26]

25. George Steiner claims, "A sentence always means more." *Real Presences* (Chicago: University of Chicago Press, 1991), 82. With his own Augustinian hermeneutical instincts engaged, Steiner warns, "The absolute decisive failing occurs when such approaches seek to formalize *meaning*, when they proceed upward from the phonetic, the lexical and the grammatic to the semantic and aesthetic" (81). We might ask Steiner, Why is this a problem? He answers, "There is always, as Blake taught, 'excess' of the signified beyond the signifier" (84).

26. Brevard S. Childs, *Old Testament Theology in a Canonical Context* (Philadelphia: Fortress, 1985), 13. The work by Gerald T. Sheppard that Childs alludes to here

The canon itself is not packaged so that its material form and internal associative dimensions have been cauterized once and for all.[27] New avenues of inquiry and fresh doors of associative reading are ever before readers of Holy Scripture.[28] The fields certainly bear the marks of heavy passage, but they remain white unto harvest.

Canonical Legacy: The Prophet as Word

The Old Testament does not hesitate to identify and narrate the human agents whom God inspires for his teaching and prophetic ministry. In other words, the Old Testament does not blush when it speaks of the human servants whom God sets apart for this particular task. We receive much about Moses the man. His story continues to provide fodder for Hollywood's imagination. We follow the tortuous and exhilarating narratives of Elijah the prophet— from the top of Mount Carmel to his hovering in a wilderness cave. Jeremiah's personal angst leaps off the page as he is weighted down under the heft of God's word. While these narratival dynamics are at play in various measures of detail, the Old Testament insists on the enduring legacy of the words delivered by these servants. Their words as God's Word extend far beyond their human existence and consciousness. A disproportionate relationship, then, exists between the words of the prophets and the prophetic personae who deliver them.

Wherever one lands on the critical matter of Isaiah's compositional history—how many Isaiahs are there?—it is noteworthy

---

is "Hearing the Voice of the Same God through Historically Dissimilar Traditions," *Interpretation* 36 (1982): 21–33.

27. The recent spate of interest in the intertextual dimension of the Hebrew Scriptures is exhibit A. By way of introduction, see Bernard M. Levinson, *Legal Revision and Religious Renewal in Ancient Israel* (Cambridge: Cambridge University Press, 2008).

28. Walter Moberly's fresh readings of Old Testament texts are a case in point: R. W. L. Moberly, *Old Testament Theology: Reading the Hebrew Bible as Christian Scripture* (Grand Rapids: Baker Academic, 2013).

that no named authorial prophet appears after chapter 39. The last we see of Isaiah the man is the scene depicting his bad news to King Hezekiah about future Babylonian invasion (39:5–8). (As an aside, readers may recall Hezekiah's chivalrous response to the bad news: At least "there will be peace and security in my days" [39:8].) After this scene, there is no more indication of a prophetic persona as author. Isaiah the prophet may hover around chapters 40–66 like a spirit. Delitzsch has a memorable description of this Isaianic phenomenon. Isaiah "floats along through the exile like a being of a higher order, like an angel of God."[29] But his person is not present. Isaiah as a prophetic book, in its portrayal of the prophet's physical presence and subsequent absence, may speak to the disproportionate relationship mentioned above between the prophetic persona and the prophet's words. In fact, the very next chapter of Isaiah provides the theological rationale.

> The grass withers, the flower fades
> > when the breath of the LORD blows on it;
> > surely the people are grass.
> The grass withers, the flower fades,
> > but the word of our God will stand forever. (Isa. 40:7–8)

In the latter half of the book of Isaiah, the central dramatic figure is not the human prophet per se but the word of God, which stands forever.[30] Grass comes and goes. So do prophets, who count their days along with the rest of creaturely humanity. But the Word

---

29. Delitzsch famously changed his mind on the compositional history of Isaiah in the fourth edition of his commentary. He sees it as likely that a pupil took on his master's mantle in extending Isaiah's prophetic word into a new moment. The pupil outdoes the master in his elevated style, according to Delitzsch. He concludes his comments on Isaiah's critical issues by claiming that subsequent authorship by an Isaianic disciple "may possibly be the case. It seems to me even probable, and almost certain, that this may be so; but indubitably certain it is not, in my opinion, and I shall die without getting over this hesitancy." Franz Delitzsch, *Biblical Commentary on the Prophecies of Isaiah* (Edinburgh: T&T Clark, 1894), 1:39. See Christopher R. Seitz, *Word without End* (Grand Rapids: Eerdmans, 1998), 177.

30. As Seitz clarifies, "Isaiah's 'persona' is not extended into chs. 40–66 except as his word finds vindication and extension through new voices, perhaps even Isaiah's

delivered by the prophet far outlasts the flowered existence of Isaiah the man, or any human prophet for that matter.

Zechariah the prophet echoes the claims of Isa. 40 at the beginning of his prophecy: "Your fathers, where are they? And the prophets, do they live forever? But my words and my statutes, which I commanded my servants the prophets, did they not overtake your fathers?" (Zech. 1:5–6). Zechariah speaks of the effective nature of the prophetic word to "overtake" or "catch up" with those who hear it, leading them to repentance.[31] Prophets do not live forever, yet the effect of their words continues to do so because the prophet's words are God's word. Many prophetic books begin with "the word of the LORD" coming to the prophet (cf. Mic. 1:1). The word of the Lord as the divine agent of God's own self-giving is generated by God's activity to and through human agents, an activity whose effect and power continue beyond the earthly existence of prophets and apostles. The prophetic word of God continues to effect repentance in the hearts of hearers around the world.

An example of Isaiah's enduring voice occurred one autumn afternoon as I sat around a kitchen table with several women from our church. They asked me to spend some time discussing the book of Isaiah with them. Afterward, I thought about Isaiah's claims in 40:7–8 in relation to our gathering in that modest setting. Here we were, millennia removed from Isaiah the prophet, hunkered down around a table, seeking to hear God's word through writing that has long outlasted its prophetic persona. Isaiah's prophetic book anticipated my time with these women of the

---

'second selves,' to use Delitzsch's phrase. It is the word of God that stands forever, not Isaiah or his 'persona' abstracted from that word" (*Word without End*, 179).

31. Boda understands נשג (*nsg*, overtake) within a covenantal context (Zech. 1:6) rather than the typical hunting context. In other words, the prophetic word and legal statutes will catch up with God's people as they render a blessing or a curse (cf. Deut. 28). Boda explains, "The divine word, either as law or prophecy, is an enduring and active force whose threats were faithfully fulfilled." Mark J. Boda, *The Book of Zechariah*, New International Commentary on the Old Testament (Grand Rapids: Eerdmans, 2016), 83.

church because even though Isaiah the prophet is long gone, his prophetic word endures forever. It anticipates all times when God's people seek to think God's thoughts after him.

Conclusion

The canon of Holy Scripture is the means by which God continues to disclose his person and will to his church. Holy Scripture's authority derives from this Christian confession of faith: "And he spoke by the prophets" or "Christ died for our sins, *according to the Scriptures*." As the cognitive and essential principles of Christian theology relate to each other, so also do the authority of Jesus and Scripture. To paraphrase Karl Barth on the subject, "There is no authority of Jesus in the church without the authority of Scripture. You cannot have the one without the other."[32] To claim Jesus as Savior and Lord necessitates an affirmation of the canonical authority of the Word that witnesses faithfully to him. We cannot have the one without the other.

A Christian confession regarding the character of canonical Scripture lends itself to a corresponding hermeneutical approach. This book is an attempt to bring this confession of faith to bear on the exegetical and critical inquiry into Scripture's material form, particularly its first part, the Old Testament. The cognitive principle of Scripture, with God as its object of inquiry, shapes the intellectual approach and method of inquiry. While all the elements of a humanly authored document are true of Holy Scripture, the ontological principle will not allow our method of reading to be hemmed in by its creaturely status. A theological account of canon confesses these human documents "are a witness forever," and seeks to read the text within the frame of its nature and role.

---

32. Barth actually wrote, "To say that Jesus Christ rules the Church is equivalent to saying that Holy Scripture rules the Church. The one explains the other, the one can only be understood through the other." Karl Barth, *Church Dogmatics*, ed. G. W. Bromiley and T. F. Torrance, trans. G. T. Thompson and H. Knight (Edinburgh: T&T Clark, 1956), I/2:693.

2

Sanding with the Grain

Final Form and Canonical Shape

What are we reading when we read the Bible? Or perhaps more precisely, what is the object and goal of our interpretive engagement with Holy Scripture? Such seemingly jejune questions are riddled with complexity on the far side of modernity's engagement with scriptural texts. Biblical books are complex textual artifacts.[1] As such, a romantic notion of authorship becomes problematic when applied to biblical texts; by comparison, William Faulkner pens *The Sound and the Fury* as an act of individual literary genius. Biblical books don't quite come to be in this fashion. In light of such textual complexity, the canonical approach helpfully clarifies the object of biblical reading and exegesis by means of two interrelated subjects. First, the final form of the text receives privileged status. For example, I am reading Isaiah as a sixty-six-chapter whole and not as a reconstructed

1. The terms *diachronic* and *synchronic* are often bandied about in biblical scholarship. Diachronic addresses the "through time," or historical, development of biblical books on their way to final production. Synchronic addresses the object of study from the standpoint of its completed and stable form.

text built on the book's complex diachronic history, while fully aware that Isaiah's diachronic history may in fact be complex. And second, the canonical shaping of the final form leaves a hermeneutical, or interpretive, stamp both on the individual parts and the whole of the text in question. These two concerns are the focal point of this chapter.

To gain clarity regarding these twin concerns, attention will be given first to a brief history of modern criticism's problematizing of the final form. Whether in source, form, or tradition-historical guise, these methods, while helpful in illuminating certain aspects of the text, run the very real risk of altering the Bible into a *source* for critical reconstruction rather than a *witness* to divine revelation. While wary of binary thinking that is too brittle to hold together a text's multifaceted complexity, the canonical approach does resist the religiohistorical instincts undergirding much of the critical project. It favors the prioritization of the canonical end for which these texts were preserved. In other words, an important distinction remains between the religio- or sociohistorical forces giving rise to biblical traditions/texts and the preservation of these texts in canonical form as a continued medium of divine self-disclosure.

The Canonical Approach in Critical Context

Brevard Childs, the founding father of the canonical hermeneutic presented here, recognizes his own approach within the strain of Old Testament criticism he learned in Germany. In the preface to his *Old Testament Theology in a Canonical Context*, Childs thanks his "unforgettable teachers," W. Eichrodt, G. von Rad, and W. Zimmerli. Von Rad and Zimmerli represent the tradition-critical approach at its apex. We will clarify these terms in due course. But at this juncture it is important to recognize Childs's training and the benefit he attached to it. Childs claims, "My sense of continuity with these great scholars of the church exceeds that of rupture."[2] At its most basic level, the canonical approach recognizes the achievements of modern criticism, resisting the easy dismissal of its textual insights because of its questionable sources (i.e., the genetic fallacy).

Still, Childs understands that the approach he is about to broker for his readership runs on a course of stated disagreement with his professors at crucial points. The canonical approach identifies itself as a broad-ranging hermeneutic whose boundaries are marked by Christian commitments. In this sense, the canonical approach recoils at its placement along a genetic linking of critical approaches, with source criticism leading to form criticism, which yields tradition criticism leading to redaction criticism and then to canonical criticism. "Rather," Childs clarifies, "the crucial issue turns on one's initial evaluation of the nature of the biblical text being studied. By defining one's task as an understanding of the Bible as the sacred Scriptures of the church, one establishes from the outset the context and point-of-understanding of the reader within the received tradition of a community of faith and practice."[3] The presupposed nature of the Old Testament as Scripture has a totalizing effect on the entire critical discipline from beginning to end. Thus the canonical approach's scope for reading provides the Christian interpreter a proper theological framework for dealing with the critical issues that pertain to the Bible's material form, even where sharp disagreements on particular critical problems remain.

A clarifying word about tradition criticism should be offered because Childs's own historical-critical training took place under the leaders of this method, as mentioned above. The canonical approach does not make sense apart from the insights garnered

2. Brevard S. Childs, *Old Testament Theology in a Canonical Context* (Philadelphia: Fortress, 1985), xiii.

3. Alan Brill, "Brevard Childs," *The Book of Doctrines and Opinions: Notes on Jewish Theology and Spirituality* (blog), April 13, 2010, https://kavvanah.wordpress.com/2010/04/13/brevard-childs/. See also Brevard S. Childs, *Introduction to the Old Testament as Christian Scripture* (Philadelphia: Fortress, 1979), 82–83.

from tradition criticism. Coming to terms, then, with tradition criticism's textual approach and insights remains an important feature of the canonical approach. Therefore, we will back into tradition criticism with a brief rehearsal of the critical approaches that preceded it.[4]

The standard critical approaches take their cue from the initial identification of literary sources in the biblical books, particularly the Pentateuch. Such findings have a long and complex history of interpretation, reaching back to the seventeenth century.[5] This literary-critical or source-critical inquiry refocused exegetical attention to the sorting out of literary sources embedded in biblical books. Such a task is more easily said than done, because the literary sources have been mixed and mingled in the books' final form. The final form of the Pentateuch, for example, needs to be sorted out to properly identify its sources. The most famous of these sources stem from the Graf-Wellhausen Documentary Hypothesis: J, E, D, and P.

A full exploration of source criticism's method, findings, and continued influence is beyond our scope at this point.[6] What should be emphasized, nevertheless, is the essential *literary* character of

4. The taxonomy of critical approaches given here is cursory at best. For a more thorough account, see John Barton, *Reading the Old Testament: Method in Biblical Study, Revised and Enlarged* (Louisville: Westminster John Knox, 1996); Odil Hannes Steck, *Old Testament Exegesis: A Guide to the Methodology*, trans. James D. Nogalski, 2nd ed. (Atlanta: Scholars Press, 1998); Mark S. Gignilliat, *A Brief History of Old Testament Criticism: From Spinoza to Childs* (Grand Rapids: Zondervan, 2012).

5. See esp. Rudolf Smend, *From Astruc to Zimmerli: Old Testament Scholarship in Three Centuries*, trans. M. Kohl (Tübingen: Mohr Siebeck, 2007).

6. It is worth pointing out that standard accounts of the Documentary Hypothesis have come under critical scrutiny, especially in European scholarship. See T. B. Dozeman and K. Schmid, eds., *Farewell to the Yahwist? The Composition of the Pentateuch in Recent European Scholarship*, SBL Symposium Series 34 (Atlanta: SBL, 2006). The assured identification of four sources (or three, if one recognizes, as Wellhausen did, that J and E were redacted together in the united monarchy, thus making their literary separation difficult, if not impossible) has fallen to a simpler P and non-P, with P understood as the literary source whose identity remains unchallenged. On the dating of P, debates continue. While most date P, as Wellhausen did, to the postexilic period, others have followed Moshe Weinfeld's rather compelling case for the preexilic character of P.

this critical approach. Properly understood from Wellhausen's perspective, the diachronic reconstruction of the Pentateuch's literary history served the greater purpose of reconstructing Israel's religious history. Still, the identification of sources was primarily a literary phenomenon. In this regard, John Barton rightly questions whether the term "historical criticism" does justice to the *literary* character of modern criticism's basic instincts.[7]

In time, and without dispensing with source criticism's findings, the *form-critical* school moved away from the identification of literary sources *back* to the oral phase of Israel's religious "traditions." This oral phase occurs within the dynamic of Israel's religious life before the sedimentation of these "traditions" took place in written form.[8] The form-critical approach sought to atomize the text into its smallest parts by identifying genres or literary forms in their pure, unmingled state. Once the interpreter identifies the form, then the original situation in life (*Sitz im Leben*) giving rise to the form becomes more apparent. For example, Ps. 2 represents a traditional form whose performance is the enthronement ritual of the ancient Israelite king. By identifying these forms, the interpreter gains purchase on a two-way interpretive street between Israel's religious experience in various historical moments and the proper understanding of the text's function. The name most often associated with form criticism

---

7. John Barton, *The Nature of Biblical Criticism* (Louisville: Westminster John Knox, 2007), 22–23. At the same time, the concern for *religiohistorical* or *empirical-historical* use of these literary findings shouldn't be underestimated, especially given the rise of historical consciousness in the late-eighteenth and nineteenth centuries. See Thomas Albert Howard, *Religion and the Rise of Historicism: W. M. L. de Wette, Jacob Burckhardt, and the Theological Origins of Nineteenth-Century Historical Consciousness* (Cambridge: Cambridge University Press, 2000). See also the discussion of historicism in later chapters.

8. The traditional genetic history of the oral phase of Israel's tradition giving way in time to their written form is no longer persuasive. With Niditch and Carr, the relation of the oral and written is now understood as existing on parallel tracks of mutual reciprocity rather than with one leading into the other. See Susan Niditch, *Oral Form and Written Word: Ancient Israelite Literature* (Louisville: Westminster John Knox, 1996); David Carr, *Writing on Tablets of the Heart: Origins of Scripture and Literature* (Oxford: Oxford University Press, 2008).

is Hermann Gunkel, a scholar whose erudition was matched by his love for the subject matter.

Tradition criticism is a species of form criticism in that it too is concerned with the oral phase of Israel's traditions and the various forms these traditions take. But instead of moving back to the original situation itself, tradition criticism concerns itself with the living dynamic of these traditions as they move forward in time and in Israel's religious consciousness.[9]

Both literary criticism and form criticism understand the pentateuchal text's final form (Genesis–Deuteronomy) as a problem to be overcome by the identification of either literary sources or religious traditions within these sources. Tradition criticism, on the other hand, attends to the text's final form because of the tradition-building process leading to it. For example, Gerhard von Rad, a leading proponent of tradition criticism, begins with the final form of the Hexateuch (Genesis–Joshua) and seeks to understand how the complex amalgamation of various blocks of tradition had their origin (form criticism) and continued developing up to the final form.[10] When von Rad turned his tradition-historical attention to the Prophets, his appreciation for the final form becomes more apparent. Here he warns against pitting "authentic" prophetic utterances against later scribal accretions, with the latter understood as theologically inferior to the former.[11]

---

9. See Douglas A. Knight, *Rediscovering the Traditions of Israel*, 3rd ed. (Atlanta: Society of Biblical Literature, 2006).

10. Von Rad begins his tradition-critical understanding of the Hexateuch with the famed three *kleines geschichtliches Credo* (small historical confessions): Deut. 26:5b–9; 6:20–24; and Josh. 24:2b–13. Norbert Lohfink's investigation into von Rad's thesis left that thesis unconvincing to most. See Gerhard von Rad, "The Form-Critical Problem of the Hexateuch," in *From Genesis to Chronicles: Explorations in Old Testament Theology*, trans. E. W. T. Dicken (Minneapolis: Fortress, 2005), 1–58.

11. Gerhard von Rad, *Old Testament Theology*, trans. D. M. G. Stalker (San Francisco: Harper & Row, 1965), 2:168:

> Critical exegesis has no great opinion of these additions or of many others like them. In so far as this verdict is literary and aesthetic, one can largely agree. The difference in the form and in force of expression is in some cases quite unmistakable: the diction is more diffuse and less colourful, it heaps up the terms used, and the result is often enough the sacrifice of clarity. Nevertheless,

---

THE CANONICAL APPROACH IN MODERN GUISE: The canonical approach is properly located on the far side of modernity's critical engagement with Scripture. While drawing on the resources and instincts of the church's premodern reading of Scripture, the canonical approach makes judicious use of modern criticism's literary engagement with the text's compositional history. The key term is *judicious* because the canonical approach makes appreciative use of critical tools while at the same time resisting modern criticism's interpretive goals and methodological hegemony.

The canonical approach breathes the air of tradition criticism's understanding of the biblical text's depth dimension. It does not shy away from an appreciation of the tradition-building process of Israel's historical traditions, prophetic utterances, cultic prayers, or wise sayings. But because the canonical approach insists on the character of Israel's Scriptures as *witness* rather than *source*, the final form of the biblical text is the privileged form. For von Rad, the final form has no particular priority over the layers of tradition identified in the compositional history of biblical books. The final form, on this account, is simply the final stage in the text's tradition-building process. A well-known example is von Rad's lionizing of the so-called Yahwist as the greatest of Israel's ancient theologians. The appreciation of the Yahwist's singular achievement demands his literary *identification* and *isolation* from its embedded literary setting. For the canonical approach, the *identification* of a source or block of tradition is one thing; its *isolation* is another.

---

we ought to exercise reserve in differentiating between what is original and what was added by successors, since the men of the ancient world were quite unfamiliar with such differentiations used as standards and measures of value. We must particularly remember that such judgments are quite meaningless as far as the theological adequacy of the additions is concerned. . . . All we can see is that the tradition of this prophet's message was not preserved in archives: it remained a living organism, speaking directly to later generations as it had done to its own, and able even of itself to give birth to new prophecy.

The So-Called Final Form

The canonical approach's identification of the text's nature as *witness* entails a high value on the biblical books' final form. The very act of preserving the biblical books and their content ensured an ongoing repository of divine revelation and self-giving. In brief, these biblical books do more than recount the religious instincts, folklore, and legal traditions of ancient Israel. Source, form, and tradition criticism instinctively understand the final form as a *source* for critical reconstruction of the text's prehistory. On these accounts, the final form presents either a hurdle to critical reconstruction or, more positively, the means for sorting out the diachronic history of the text. Yet without this reconstructed diachronic history, the texts in their given forms remain elusive. Not so with the canonical approach.

For the approach offered here, the "obstacles" that the final form presents are not hurdles that must be jumped. In fact, the final form of the text "subordinate[s], modifie[s], or place[s] in the distant background" certain features of the tradition when brought into canonical proximity and unity with other traditions.[12] The "Yahwist," for example, or "First Isaiah," by way of another example, no longer exists as such within the final presentation of the material. Nor, crucially, was their preservation within the respective biblical books "housing" them intended to preserve them in such form. They have been recalibrated and refitted canonically so that their voices register in concert with others.[13] Another way of put-

---

12. Childs, *Canonical Context*, 11.

13. For clarity's sake, it should be stated here that not much is attached to the critical conclusions assumed by most scholars. The issues do not trade at this moment in the argument on the acceptance of critical insights, moving targets that they are. Even if, say, someone affirms the unity of Isaiah on the basis of singleness of authorship (fully aware that Isaianic unity can be conceived along different lines), few who hold a single-author viewpoint assume that Isaiah was his own redactor (Calvin did not, for example!). In other words, the disparate collection of oracles, narrative literature, prophetic invectives, etc. that may all be traced to the eighth-century prophet had to be put together in some shape. Moreover, there is internal evidence suggesting that Isaiah was not the one who did this but disciples coming after him (Isa. 8:16;

TEXTUAL FINAL FORM: While recognizing a text's "depth dimension," the canonical approach privileges the literary final form of biblical books. Such a prioritization makes sense within a theological frame of God's providential ordering of time and his revelation in it. The final form also leaves an interpretive imprint on the text, rendering the whole as more than the sum total of its parts; it is the culmination of God's revealed word in time, and renders an authoritative frame of reference for the parts leading to the whole—a *witness* to God's revelation rather than a *source* for critical reconstruction.

---

ting the matter is that the canonical approach opposes too sharp a divide between text and reception. The reception of the material in canonical form leaves a permanent hermeneutical imprint on that material. I will return to this later because it is of some consequence.

A certain kind of historical consciousness undergirds these canonical instincts. Far from being uninterested in history, the canonical approach draws attention to the real importance of history theologically understood. "The significance of the final form of the biblical text," Childs claims, "is that it alone bears witness to the full history of encounter as an enduring word for future generations."[14] Childs clarifies, "It is only the final form of the biblical text in which the normative history has reached an end that the full effects of this revelatory history can be perceived."[15] In this sense, the final-form presentation functions as "a commentary on the text's prehistory."[16] Not quick to dismiss a text's prehis-

---

30:8). The shaping of Isaiah's oracles into the written form in which we have them is a first-order hermeneutical matter not solved by appeal to single authorship, e.g., the Immanuel materials' canonical significance when the totality of Isa. 7–9 is taken into account. All this is to say that redaction-critical concerns do not allow for quick dismissal even by those who affirm traditional authorship.

14. Childs, *Introduction*, 75–76.

15. Childs, *Introduction*, 76.

16. Christopher Seitz, "Canonical Approach," in *Dictionary for Theological Interpretation of the Bible*, ed. K. J. Vanhoozer (Grand Rapids: Baker Academic, 2005), 100.

tory, the canonical approach understands a textual maturity in the composition, arranging, and reception of the biblical books that should be properly understood in light of a providential account of time.

Hermeneutical Imprint

As mentioned above, the final form of the biblical books leaves a hermeneutical imprint on the biblical material. While appreciative of the depth dimension of biblical books and cognizant of the complexity of their compositional history, a canonical approach does not understand a book like Isaiah as the sum total of its composite parts. First Isaiah's message is added to Second Isaiah's, with Third Isaiah's addition rounding things off, all understood within the relative independence of their parts. Wellhausen's *Prolegomena to the History of Israel* begins section 2 with a quote from the Greek poet Hesiod: "The half is more than the whole."[17] Quite to the contrary, the canonical approach understands the whole as more than the sum of its parts. Not only is the whole more than the half, the whole is more than the two halves combined. The final selection and arranging of the parts provides an interpretive lens for how one understands the book as a whole.[18]

By way of illustration, I will expand on the previous comments about Isaiah. The standard critical view dates First Isaiah (chaps. 1–39) to the eighth-century prophet Isaiah. Put better,

17. Hesiod, *Works and Days* 40, quoted in Julius Wellhausen, *Prolegomena to the History of Israel*, trans. J. S. Black and A. Menzies (Atlanta: Scholars Press, 1994), 169. This quote reveals Wellhausen's understanding of the development of ancient Judaism from an intuitive, religious body living in relative freedom from institutional norms into a postexilic community where the aridity of institutional life had taken over.

18. For clarity's sake, this understanding of the selection and arranging of materials does not trade on traditional views of authorship versus critical views. For on both accounts, the biblical books' arrangement comes after the stated author of the book. A key example of this with Isaiah is the intertextual relation between chaps. 1 and 66. See H. G. M. Williamson, *Isaiah 1–5*, International Critical Commentary (London: T&T Clark International, 2006), ad loc.

the eighth-century prophet is found only in the corpus of First Isaiah, yet the critical view recognizes later additions within these chapters as well, such as the so-called Isaiah apocalypse (Isa. 24–27). Second Isaiah (chaps. 40–55) has its provenance in the Babylonian exile of the sixth century; Third Isaiah (chaps. 56–66) emerged in postexilic Yehud. There are good reasons why some critical scholars doubt the literary integrity of a Third Isaiah, but that question is beside the point here.[19] The canonical approach does not resist a diachronic understanding of Isaiah's compositional history along critical lines, even as certain aspects of this history continue to be debated. The approach may register its complaints about a standard Duhmian[20] view of Isaiah's compositional history—that the three Isaiahs originated independently from each other—but that Isaiah is composite or has material that postdates the eighth-century author is not ruled out of court. In fact, it is assumed.

At the same time, the canonical approach understands the final shaping of the book within a sixty-six-chapter whole as leaving an indelible imprint on the various parts and the historical accidents giving rise to their production. For example, even if Isa. 40–55 is born out of Babylonian provenance—whether by a later prophet/ Isaianic disciple (as held by Franz Delitzsch)[21] or by Isaiah's own clairvoyant state into a future time (proposed by John Oswalt)[22]— the fitting of Isa. 40–55 within the larger sixty-six-chapter complex loosens the text from its original historical moorings as it is brought into concert with the book's broad and multilayered sweep. The implications of this canonical understanding have broad and particular effects. They are broad in that the hearing

19. Benjamin D. Sommer, *A Prophet Reads Scripture: Allusion in Isaiah 40–66* (Stanford, CA: Stanford University Press, 1998), 4–5.

20. Bernhard Duhm, *Das Buch Jesaia, übersetzt und erklärt*, Handkommentar zum Alten Testament (Göttingen: Vandenhoeck & Ruprecht, 1892).

21. Franz Delitzsch, *Biblical Commentary on the Prophecies of Isaiah* (Edinburgh: T&T Clark, 1894).

22. John N. Oswalt, *The Book of Isaiah*, 2 vols., New International Commentary on the Old Testament (Grand Rapids: Eerdmans, 1986, 1998).

of the whole book as an enduring word requires more from the reader than historical excavation. It requires the reader to listen patiently to the whole of the text in light of its parts, and this despite the possibility of multiple historical particularities in the text. Likewise, the effect is particular in that the parts are now to be heard in light of the whole. This is the canonical effect of the book's final form as it makes its claims on the whole and the parts. Moreover, this canonical effect is not a tack-on that is extraneous to the biblical material, a kind of external decision to understand Isaiah in this way. Quite the opposite is the case. Embedded within the material itself is an understanding of the text's enduring character as a witness, which has pressured internal decisions regarding the book's movement toward final form and stabilization. The term associated with this dynamic is "canon consciousness" (*Kanonsbewusstsein*).

Within the Isaianic corpus, one of the more important, or at least familiar, texts affected by this canonical understanding is Isa. 7:14. Here the prophet Isaiah gives an unasked-for sign to Ahaz the king: "This shall be a sign unto you: a virgin shall conceive and bear a son, and you shall call his name Immanuel" (my trans.). Along form-critical grounds one could argue that a promised sign to Ahaz that awaits fulfillment until the time of Jesus makes no sense. One could also argue that a sign, whether it was Isaiah's child (Isa. 8) or Ahaz's son Hezekiah, was given to Ahaz within his historical frame so that he could presumably point and say, "He is the sign." But the canonical approach resists the atomizing instincts of form criticism that tend toward an overly historicized understanding of the biblical text, even if this history is *religious* and not *empirical*. Why would the canonical approach resist this flat account of the text? Because within the canonical shape of Isaiah, Isa. 7 no longer functions as a stand-alone text reporting a historical encounter. It is now fitted into the larger "Immanuel" context of chapters 8–9, with the child imagery of 9:6 coming to bear on our understanding of the eschatological implications of the promised sign.[23] Within its canonical context Isa. 7 now does more than report a historical encounter between Isaiah and Ahaz. To be clear, it does not do less than give us a record of this encounter, but its canonical role does more than this, as particular symbolic encounters are wed to larger contextual and theological networks.

The textual illustration chosen here is Isaiah, a book whose critical issues are the stuff of continued disagreement within confessional settings to this day. Yet the implications of the final form go beyond Isaiah to every quarter of the Old Testament. The canonical shape of the Pentateuch as a five-book Torah collection differs from von Rad's Hexateuch (Genesis–Joshua, with Joshua understood as rounding off Deuteronomy)[24] or Martin Noth's Tetrateuch (Genesis–Numbers, with Deuteronomy and the Deuteronomistic history—Joshua to Kings—understood as coming from a single pen and embodying a shared theological outlook).[25] For that matter, the canonical approach grows uneasy with David Noel Freedman's "great history" of Genesis to Kings, if this "great history" attenuates the significance of the division between Deuteronomy and Joshua.[26] The canonical approach takes the division between Deuteronomy and Joshua seriously, because the text itself, in Joshua, takes the division seriously. *And* this division has hermeneutical significance as it illustrates the reciprocal relationship between the Law and the Prophets. The division of the Prophets leans on the anterior authority of the Law. And the Prophetic division of the canon also helps us understand

23. The implications of this canonical reading for how we understand prophetic fulfillment are noteworthy. On this account, fulfillment is not a mortar shot from text to Jesus Christ. The etymology of the term *fulfillment* comes into play at this point. Prophecy, like Isa. 7:14, is "filled to its fullness" in the person and work of Jesus Christ. But this does not rule out the possibility of previous fulfillments en route to a prophecy's ultimate filling out in the person and work of Jesus Christ.

24. Von Rad, "Form-Critical Problem of the Hexateuch."

25. Martin Noth, *A History of Pentateuchal Traditions*, trans. Bernhard W. Anderson (Englewood Cliffs, NJ: Prentice-Hall, 1972).

26. David Noel Freedman, *The Unity of the Hebrew Bible* (Ann Arbor: University of Michigan Press, 1991).

the implications and interpretation of the Law in Israel's lived encounter with Yhwh.

A point of clarification is needed here. When delving into the scholarly literature, one becomes aware that critical scholarship understands the traditions embedded in the text's final form to reveal the religiohistorical diversity, complexity, and disagreements of ancient Israel at various moments in its history. A student may read of a "debate" between Micah and Isaiah on the nature of the future kingdom of peace.[27] Or a student may come across research on monotheism in ancient Israel only to find out that monotheism as we typically understand it—only one God exists—may not be the monotheism of the Old Testament, or at least the Old Testament in its entirety.[28] Pentateuchal scholarship has long pointed out the very different views between the so-called Priestly strand and Deuteronomy. The Priestly tradition views Israel's religious life from the vantage point of the temple and has this cultic orientation as its major theme. Deuteronomy has a broader view of Torah's implications, thus considering not only cultic/religious concerns but civic and political matters as well. Weinfeld understands the literary phenomenon to reveal the different social settings from which the literature emerges.[29] The Priestly literature has its source in the temple scribes. Deuteronomy's sociohistorical

27. E.g., Marvin A. Sweeney, *Form and Intertextuality in Prophetic and Apocalyptic Literature*, Forschungen zum Alten Testament 45 (Tübingen: Mohr Siebeck, 2005), 210–21.

28. E.g., Benjamin D. Sommer, *The Bodies of God and the World of Ancient Israel* (Cambridge: Cambridge University Press, 2009), 145–74; see also Sommer's helpful chapter "Monotheism," in *The Hebrew Bible: A Critical Companion*, ed. J. Barton (Princeton: Princeton University Press, 2016), 239–70.

29. Moshe Weinfeld, *Deuteronomy and the Deuteronomic School* (Winona Lake, IN: Eisenbrauns, 1992), 179–89. Karel van der Toorn believes the distinction between royal scribes and priestly scribes is overwrought. In fact, he argues that the temple scribes, rather than the so-called royal scribes (more "secretaries of state" than literary agents), are the Hebrew Bible's "likely center of production." Van der Toorn also believes the so-called "ideological" differences between palace and temple reflect a poor historical understanding of the insoluble link between church and state. See his *Scribal Culture and the Making of the Hebrew Bible* (Cambridge, MA: Harvard University Press, 2007), 82–89.

provenance is the royal court. On sociological grounds, interpreters can make sense of the distinctive theological outlooks emerging from the literature.

All of the critical issues in the previous paragraph are matters of continued scholarly investigation. Critical consensus is more often than not the unicorn in the woods. Therefore, the matters above are mentioned only illustratively to clarify what the canonical approach is about, especially in light of socio- or religiohistorical knowledge. Still, the canonical approach does not resist seeing social or religious complexity as the historical phenomenon behind the Bible's production. For any student of church history, this should come as no surprise. God's providential oversight of creaturely affairs toward his own end does not necessarily place a halo on people or institutions. The author of this book is thoroughly Cyrillian in his Christology, resisting the Nestorian tendency to treat the two natures of Christ apart from each other. At the same time, Cyril of Alexandria's borderline Machiavellian political maneuvering for the dominance of his viewpoint cannot be easily dismissed. Cyril proved to be an irascible and calculating fellow. In other words, providence does not remove creaturely messiness.

At the same time, and moreover, the canonical approach makes an important distinction between the religio- or sociohistorical realities behind the text that gave rise to the diversity of Israel's traditions and the Scripture's canonical function as a received text. The waters we are navigating at this point begin to churn. The canonical approach does not deny complexity or theological diversity in Israel's religious history: for example, the scribal culture of the temple strikes a different theological chord than the theological views coming from the royal court. Again, the canonical approach clarifies the basic issue at stake, with its differentiation between the Scriptures as *source* or as *witness*. Put in historical terms, the motivation compelling the scribal culture of ancient Israel to preserve its various traditions in canonical form was not for the sake of preserving the religiohistorical diversity of ancient

Israel: an impulse having more in common with modern notions of religious plurality, which on first and second hearing would strike the temple scribes as foreign.[30]

The canon's authoritative understanding and preservation of the diversity of Israel's oral and written traditions place the emphasis elsewhere. The diversity of views and inner complexity of the Old Testament's self-witness reveals the multifaceted character of the Old Testament's subject matter—as with the Gospels in the New Testament, so too with the Old Testament. Given the subject matter of Scripture, a diversity of views need not be understood on final analysis as an internal contradiction but as a complex and expected necessity, given Scripture's subject matter: God, his people, and the world.

Admittedly, the dangers in this discussion lurk in the generalities. These governing instincts need to be worked out on the ground floor.[31] The canonical instinct to hear a unified chorus of voices in Scripture does not mean that the choir sings melody only. Its harmonies, in fact, are more like complex and intricate choral music (think of Gabriel Fauré's *Requiem*), not the catchy but simple melodies of a praise chorus (no disrespect toward praise choruses intended!). In other words, the hard work of exegesis and inner-associative readings are not done away with because the canonical approach does not pit the various traditions of Scripture against each other. One could argue that the identification of the Old Testament's diversity is the easier enterprise. Seeking to hear the Old Testament's symphonic voice as a single and yet complex phenomenon may be the harder task.[32]

30. For example, Weinfeld helps us understand that for all the diversity of views between P and Deuteronomy, the views need not be understood as incompatible.

31. Childs, *Introduction*, 78.

32. "This potential for multilayered reading of a biblical text has not been obliterated by its final canonical form, but rather placed within certain canonical restrictions. The exegete is thus given the challenge by the form of the text itself neither to flatten its voice into a monotone, nor to claim such signs of dissonance within the levels of the text as to call into question any coherent meaning or authoritative role within a community of faith." Brevard S. Childs, *Biblical Theology of the Old*

A Judicious Use of Critical Scholarship

Much of the above discussion reveals the canonical approach's indebtedness to the critical tradition. While embracing the hermeneutical and theological instincts of premodern exegetes such as Luther or Calvin when it comes to Scripture's nature and subject matter, it must be stressed that the canonical approach resides on the far side of modernity. It is not merely an atavistic retrieval of a better day when things were much simpler. Aspects of the approach would not make sense to a Luther or Calvin, given their place in the history of ideas, though Calvin's views on the authorship of Joshua and 2 Peter reveal his own critical faculties at work. Equally, the canonical approach's relationship to modern criticism is uneasy because it resists the hegemony of historical criticism as typically practiced by scholars. A residual tension remains in the canonical approach's relation to historical criticism. The tension surfaces in the work of Childs, and an example of this tension illustrates the point at hand.

Childs affirms a depth dimension to the biblical books. Such has been the claim of this chapter. But Childs also sits loosely regarding the ability of critical scholars to make assured claims about the diachronic history of biblical books. "That the final form of the biblical text has preserved much from the earliest stages of Israel's theological reflection is fully evident. However, the various elements have been so fused as to resist easy diachronic reconstructions which fracture the witness as a whole."[33] Crucial terms in this warning of Childs are "easy" and "fracture." Again, Childs makes use of critical scholarship, and more than this, is a very proficient critical scholar himself, as shown by his commentaries on Exodus and Isaiah.[34] But Childs understands that those

---

and New Testaments: Theological Reflection on the Christian Bible (Minneapolis: Fortress, 1992), 105.

33. Childs, *Canonical Context*, 11.

34. See Stephen B. Chapman, "Brevard Childs as a Historical Critic: Divine Concession and the Unity of the Canon," in *The Bible as Christian Scripture: The Work*

who treasured and shaped the biblical books of the Old Testament canon covered their tracks in such a way as to make historical reconstruction of the text's prehistory nearly impossible to do with precision. Broad brush strokes may be in order here or there (and even these broad-brush strokes are amendable), but detailed diachronic reconstructions that confidently assign various layers of the text to different historical periods of the text's compositional history make for a tall order.[35]

Childs also calls into question the governing logic of certain redaction critics and the means by which they identify seams in the prophetic literature. Different layers of the prophetic literature are identified by supposed conceptual tensions. The identification of these tensions provides the empirical evidence necessary for confident identification of redactional layers. For example, the presentation of the "servant" in Isa. 40–55 leaves the reader caught between a corporate and an individual understanding of the servant figure. Thus a conceptual tension is present in the material that begs to be explained by assigning the texts in tension to different redactional levels. Childs retorts, "The problem with this newer redactional analysis is that under the guise of diversity the biblical text is subjected to the criteria of rigorous, conceptual coherence which has been defined according to modern rational categories."[36] In other words, a modern account of conceptual coherence may be an imposition onto the authors and shapers of the biblical material. What may seem conceptually incoherent to us may not be so in the historical frame of the Old Testament's composition and formation.

---

of *Brevard S. Childs*, ed. Christopher R. Seitz and Kent Harold Richards (Atlanta: Society of Biblical Literature, 2013), 63–84.

35. Benjamin D. Sommer, who himself works with critical categories in his scholarship, labels the confident identification of a text's historical provenance as "pseudo-historicism." "Dating Pentateuchal Texts and the Perils of Pseudo-Historicism," in *The Pentateuch: International Perspectives on Current Research*, Forschungen zum Alten Testament 71 (Tübingen: Mohr Siebeck, 1998), 85–108.

36. Brevard S. Childs, "Retrospective Reading of the Old Testament Prophets," *Zeitschrift für die alttestamentliche Wissenschaft* 108 (1996): 369.

Childs also leans against synchronic readings of Scripture that do not seek to do justice at some level to the diachronic realities of the text's prehistory. The tension in Childs resides precisely at this point, and it is perhaps why readers find him frustrating at times. In his *Biblical Theology* the following claim is made:

> Thus it greatly sharpens one's vision of the final form of the Penta-teuch which is the goal of exegesis if one first distinguishes between earlier and later levels within the witness. To shift the imagery, one can better appreciate a symphony if one has been trained to recognize the contribution of each of the various musical instruments involved. The crucial test is the extent to which the recognition of the parts aids rather than impairs the hearing of the whole.[37]

The felt tension between Childs's misgivings about reconstructing a detailed diachronic history and his affirmation of the herme-neutical value of doing so at some level are not easily resolved. Certainly Childs the practitioner showed good instincts in the judicious use of critical tools. But perhaps the tension should not be resolved theoretically but worked out in the practice of biblical exegesis. At the same time, Childs had no misgivings about the ends toward which critical tools are used: as an aid to hearing the final form of the text well. Childs's clarity on the goal of such critical utilization comes from his commitment to reading the Old Testament as witness to God's identity and ways with his people.

Canonical Shaping and the Book of the Twelve

For some time now, Old Testament scholarship has given attention to the unity of the Minor Prophets, or the Book of the Twelve. By means of identifying the close links between the ends and begin-nings of books (e.g., Amos ends with an oracle against Edom, giv-ing way to Obadiah's one-chapter focus on Edom) and internal in-tertextual dynamics (e.g., the leitmotif of the *middot* [attributes]

37. Childs, *Biblical Theology*, 105.

of God in Exod. 34:6–7 and running through the Twelve at various junctures), scholars have given attention to the internal prophetic conversation at play in the Minor Prophets' coming to be. Something is happening on the compositional level of these books that encourages readers to read them in conversation with one another.

The recognition of these internal dynamics does not diminish the legitimacy of reading the individual voices of the Twelve as unique testimonies. Commentaries on Amos, for example, should continue to roll off the press. Contrary to some redaction-critical strategies for reading the Twelve, the integrity of the individual books should be maintained rather than assigning various redactional levels of, for example, Amos or Micah to a reconstructed religiohistorical development. Yet at the same time, an attentiveness to the Twelve's canonical shape provides avenues of theological and textual insight that may stimulate deeper appreciation for the individual voices present within the Twelve's overall scope when these books are brought into conversation with one another.

For example, and as already mentioned above, the attributes of Yhwh's name given to Moses after the golden-calf debacle make their way through the Twelve at critical junctures (Exod. 34:6–7).[38] The attributes reveal Yhwh's character as merciful and severe, with these two attributes stemming from the singularity of God's being. With the redemptive context of the Prophets, as observed figurally in the golden-calf narratives of Exodus, Yhwh's severity/justice opens up to the future of his forgiveness, mercy, and healing. Within the frame of Exodus, these attributes attest to Yhwh's forgiveness of his people and his resolving not to destroy them despite their immediate breaking of the first commandment.

---

38. See Raymond C. Van Leeuwen, "Scribal Wisdom and Theodicy in the Book of the Twelve," in *In Search of Wisdom: Essays in Memory of John G. Gammie*, ed. L. G. Perdue, B. B. Scott, and W. J. Wiseman (Louisville: Westminster John Knox, 1993), 31–49; Christopher R. Seitz, *Prophecy and Hermeneutics: Toward a New Introduction to the Prophets*, Studies in Theological Interpretation (Grand Rapids: Baker Academic, 2007).

Within the Twelve, the *middot* provide a critical and theological handle for coming to terms with Hosea's hermeneutical invitation at the end of his book:

> Those who are wise understand these things;
>   those who are discerning know them.
> For the ways of the LORD are right,
>   and the upright walk in them,
>   but transgressors stumble in them. (Hosea 14:9 NRSV)

The *middot* from Exodus help readers navigate the "discerning . . . of the LORD" and his ways.

The attributes appear in Joel 2, Jon. 4, Mic. 7, and Nah. 1, with the latter attesting to the eventual severity of God against Nineveh. God's severity against the "anti-elect," to borrow Joel Kaminksy's category, is received as divine grace for those who have suffered under their terror (cf. Ps. 73).[39] The canonical shaping and interrelatedness of these sections provides a portrait of God's relationship to Israel and the nations: Yhwh is patient and merciful, yet his patience is not boundless in the face of persistent rebellion.[40] Ask the Ninevites. Ask Israel. Ask Judah. The attributes also attest that repentance remains a live possibility for all of humanity because genuine repentance always leads to a merciful end. Ask the Ninevites in Jonah. Ask Judah. Ask the Church.

Conclusion

The tension felt in the canonical approach's relationship to biblical criticism might leave those unfamiliar with critical approaches or immediately resistant to them with a bad taste. While this resistance is understandable, the canonical approach does make

39. Joel S. Kaminsky, *Yet I Loved Jacob: Reclaiming the Biblical Concept of Election* (Nashville: Abingdon, 2007).

40. See Christopher R. Seitz, *Prophecy and Hermeneutics: Toward a New Introduction to the Prophets* (Grand Rapids: Baker Academic, 2007), 147–48.

a distinction between the reality of a depth dimension and the confidence often attached to critical conclusions. Recognizing that there is a depth dimension to a book like Psalms and reconstructing this depth dimension in detail are two related but distinct things. Moreover, the canonical approach works with theological categories: the governing standpoint of divine providence in creaturely affairs, the enduring character of the divine word, and its application into new situations in Israel's life. This top-down approach to biblical criticism makes no sense apart from theological commitments on the front end of the critical task. And in this vein, it differs significantly from a bottom-up, or *religiohistorical*, approach to critical issues, even when the latter provides helpful material with which to work.

Perhaps Christopher Seitz says it best when he identifies the canonical approach this way: "Canonical reading is therefore not an exact science, but a theological decision about what the proper parameters for interpretation are: the final form presentation and the arrangement and sequencing that it exhibits, over against the simple history of the text's development as this is critically reconstructed."[41] Far from cutting off the exegetical enterprise, the canonical approach provides a theological framework and green light for continued reading of Holy Scripture in anticipation of hearing God's Word once again.

---

41. Seitz, "Canonical Approach," 101.

3

Canonical Intentionality

The current chapter expands on the previous one by examining more closely the relationship between intentionality and canon. Admittedly, critical inquiry into authorial intentionality or textual intentionality opens up a veritable Pandora's box. This chapter, therefore, makes no claim to coverage, exhaustive or otherwise, of this complex hermeneutical matter. What this chapter does seek to do is situate the canonical approach within a hermeneutical frame that, on the one hand, denies the indeterminate character of biblical texts and, on the other, affirms modern criticism's problematizing of any simple, romantic understanding of authorial agency.

Who is the "author" of Chronicles, Job, numerous Psalms, and Joshua? And the list could continue. The straightforward identification of biblical authors with the books that bear their name is also problematized on multiple fronts: what about tradents, editors, and scribes? For example, who put together the Psalms in the canonical shape it has taken, and what was their reason for doing so? This simplistic framing of the question concerning authorship in the Old Testament and our oft-repeated inability to identify authors only highlights the problem. The interpretive problem surfaces quickly. How does the canon of Scripture maintain its identity as an object without being subsumed into the consciousness of its reader if authorial identification appears to remain at arm's length? Equally, how does the affirmation of a reader's historical and social particularity not necessarily lead to Scripture's becoming a wax nose fitted to the conscious or subconscious ideology of particular social groups of readers?

These kinds of questions about texts, intentionality, authors, readers, and cultural and ideological differences lead inquirers into the complex terrain of one of the twentieth and twenty-first centuries' most vexing philosophical challenges, especially given the prominence of the philosophy of language in the Anglo-speaking world.[1] The canonical approach does not hover above these philosophical challenges. At times even the canonical approach has been labeled New Criticism hiding under a nom de plume.[2] Nevertheless, the canonical approach resists facile associations with a particular literary-critical or philosophical point of view because its governing instincts are theological in character from beginning to end.

1. The chapter on exegetical metaphysics will more closely explore the relation between biblical language and metaphysical commitments.

2. See John Barton, *Reading the Old Testament: Method in Biblical Study*, rev. and enlarged ed. (Louisville: Westminster John Knox, 1996), chap. 10. A simple definition of New Criticism is the recognition that textual intentionality is located internally, in the given evidence of the text itself, not in the psychology of the author (the intentional fallacy) or the sincerity of the reader/critic (the affective fallacy). Quoting William Wimsatt, Deborah Bowen claims that "the first 'begins by trying to derive the standard of criticism from the psychological *causes* of the poem and ends in biography and relativism,' whereas the second 'begins by trying to derive the standard of criticism from the psychological effects of the poem and ends in impressionism and relativism.'" Wimsatt, *The Verbal Icon: Studies in the Meaning of Poetry* (Lexington: University of Kentucky Press, 1954), 21; Bowen, "Wimsatt, William Kurtz, Jr.," in *Encyclopedia of Contemporary Literary Theory: Approaches, Scholars, Terms*, ed. I. R. Makaryk (Toronto: University of Toronto Press, 1993), 492. A "canonical" text for this movement is the oft-cited article by J. K. Wimsatt and Monroe C. Beardsley, "The Intentional Fallacy," *Sewanee Review*, no. 4 (1946): 468–88. For a helpful survey of the issues related to postmodern hermeneutics and a clearing away of common misunderstandings, see Merold Westphal, *Whose Community? Which Interpretation? Philosophical Hermeneutics for the Church*, The Church and Postmodern Culture (Grand Rapids: Baker Academic, 2009).

At the same time, the canonical approach does not divest itself of interest in "intention" or "authors."[3] With modern criticism, the canonical approach does not work with a simplistic notion of authorship—that the books in the form we have them have been written and shaped by the authorial names associated with their books, such as Isaiah or Jeremiah. As mentioned in the previous chapter, even John Calvin made an effort to give an account of how the oracles of Isaiah, once treasured and housed in the temple, came to be in the canonical form of the book we now know. Calvin did not think Isaiah did this. Neither did the Talmud in its oft-repeated claim in Bava Batra 14–15 that the "Sons of Hezekiah" wrote (כתב) the book of Isaiah. The canonical process that moves toward literary stabilization problematizes any simple or overly romantic understanding of authorship. Such is the case despite one's view on authorship in the more narrow sense, such as holding that all the oracles of Isaiah originate in some sense with Isaiah the eighth-century prophet. Calvin is a case in point. Despite the problems for intentionality created by modern criticism, the canonical approach does not jettison a concern for it.

Without getting bogged down in the minutiae of philosophical or historical-critical disputation, the canonical approach recognizes the following features of the biblical books: the texts of the Old Testament are complex, spanning different times and outlooks, both in the whole and in individual books themselves; this compositional reality makes the identification of authorial intentionality difficult, even at times impossible, to do with precision. Multiple "intentionalities" may be at play within one particular book. For example, Jeremiah is not a book that has the historical scope of Isaiah. It covers the generations during the late preexilic

---

3. The increased discomfort Childs expressed concerning Walter Brueggemann's postmodern approach illustrates the misgivings Childs had about this hermeneutical direction. He expressed similar concerns about Hans Frei's understanding of the literal sense of Scripture as inseparable from the community of faith's *use* of it: the postliberal indebtedness to Ludwig Wittgenstein's language, as used within the language games of a particular culture, is readily observed.

and the exilic periods. Still, interpreters to this day struggle with relating the prophetic, narrative, and sermonic elements of the book within a single frame of intentionality. John Bright once described Jeremiah as "a hopeless hodgepodge thrown together without any discernible principle of arrangement at all."[4]

Therefore the canonical approach's registered concern for an "intentionality" of some sort is not an intentionality that derives from a purely historical-descriptive or literary-genetic account: intentionality located specifically in the immediate textual origins of original author and original audience. Within this conception of intentionality, texts are historically located by a projected *Tendenz* (point of view or purpose) that allows the interpreter to identify the literary source or "author" of the text and its immediate audience. Historical criticism and the concern for authorial intentionality are kissing cousins, even if the former has made the identification of the latter more difficult.

The canonical approach, on the other hand, conceives of intentionality more broadly as it identifies the authorial voice of the text with its final form, along with its privileged arrangement and deployment of texts, traditions, or prophetic oracles whose initial intention(s) may have had a more narrow range of effects. One could construe intentionality of this kind as "thick" rather than "thin." A thin account locates intentionality within a narrow frame of individual authorship. A thick account takes into view a providentially constructed understanding of history where a wide range of historical figures and inspired words are deemed relevant to the texts as they come to their full form. The term associated with this particular understanding is *canonical intentionality*.[5]

4. John Bright, *Jeremiah*, Anchor Bible 21 (Garden City, NY: Doubleday, 1965), lvi.

5. Seitz claims, "Whatever else might be said about Childs's approach, he clearly has an enlarged and sophisticated notion of authorial intention. He depends upon a view of revelation in history that begins with events and their immediate interpretation, but also looks to the divine word as received by the community of faith, reheard and reshaped, continuing to call forth new theological insight, obedience, and a life of faith congruent with the divine will." Christopher R. Seitz, *Word without End: The Old Testament as Abiding Theological Witness* (Grand Rapids: Eerdmans, 1998), 80.

Canonical Intentionality in Critical Discussion

What critical investigation of Israel's Scriptures reveals, even where details of the critical project are disputed, is that the reconstruction of the literary process defies simplistic solutions.[6] How the canonical texts moved toward final literary stabilization is continued fodder for scholarly dispute because of the scant nature of the evidence. Childs describes the religiohistorical phenomenon thus: "Beginning in the pre-exilic period, but increasing in significance in the post-exilic era, a force was unleashed by Israel's religious use of her traditions which exerted an influence on the shaping of the literature as it was selected, collected and ordered."[7] Various religious and political groups may have been the immediate cause of the ordering and selecting of Israel's traditions. Childs remains comfortable in identifying some of these groups with the standard critical categories, such as the Deuteronomic party or the Hezekian party. "But," Childs maintains, "basic to the canonical process is that those responsible for the actual editing of the text did their best to obscure their own identity."[8] In other words, the sociological realities requisite for any attempt to recover an author or editor's *intention*, however naive such attempts are philosophically or hermeneutically, become sand slipping through the fingers. Any attempt to identify authorial intentionality securely runs into enormous problems that the canon itself creates: the editors of the biblical material operated in a religious tradition that was

6. David Carr explains much in his understanding of the parallel lives of the oral and written phases of ancient literature. Rather than orality leading genetically to a written medium, Carr understands the two as mutually influencing in parallel. See *Writing on the Tablet of the Heart: Origins of Scripture and Literature* (Oxford: Oxford University Press, 2005). The various phases of biblical books resist the notion of simple linear development. See also Walter J. Ong, *Orality and Literacy: The Technologizing of the Word* (1982; 2nd ed., New York: Routledge, 2002). Ong also shows how the oral, more naturally fitted to human communication, and writing, not necessarily natural to discourse, relate to one another in literate cultures (see esp. chap. 4 of *Orality and Literacy*).

7. Brevard S. Childs, *Introduction to the Old Testament as Christian Scripture* (Philadelphia: Fortress, 1979), 78.

8. Childs, *Introduction*, 78.

CANONICAL INTENTIONALITY: The canonical approach conceives of the text's intentionality in the authorial voice of the text's final form. While the religiohistorical phenomena producing the various canonical voices are not denied, the canonical approach understands the text's intentionality as "loosened" from these historical forces for the sake of an enduring witness to divine self-revelation.

theocentric rather than anthropocentric in their conception of authorship.

Recent work on the formation of the Hebrew Bible leans against older genetic theories of Israel's literature that understood the oral character of Israel's tradition giving way in time to the written form: the oral traditions move in a singular direction toward the static or written. On the basis of comparative analogies within the ancient Near Eastern and Greco-Roman literary phenomena, newer theories suggest the oral and written phases of Israel's tradition more likely took place on parallel historical tracks, with each mutually informing the other for the sake of continued performance.[9] While this historical description of the literary history of Israel's Scripture may have much to commend it, the canonical approach recognizes that "the actual process by which the text was reworked lies in almost total obscurity."[10]

Therefore, "intentionality" of the Hebrew Scriptures registers its force apart from the reconstruction of the literary process itself or the various reconstructions of sociological realities that gave rise to the surplus of traditions embedded in the final form of the Hebrew Scriptures. While fully affirming of the socio- and religiohistorical realities behind biblical language, Childs still maintains

9. David Carr identifies this tradition-transmission dynamic as "oral-written, cognitive transmission" with certain variants of these traditions understood as "memory variants" typical of texts transmitted through memory, whether oral or written. *The Formation of the Hebrew Bible: A New Reconstruction* (Oxford: Oxford University Press, 2011), chap. 1.

10. Childs, *Introduction*, 78.

that intentionality understood within the reconstruction of these socio- and religiohistorical verities "runs directly in the face of the canon's intention."[11]

Canon, Community, and Anticipated Readers

A significant claim of the canonical approach trades on the issues briefly addressed above: the insoluble and dialectical relationship between an understanding of the canon's intention and the community of faith that received and treasured the Scriptures as a sacred text. The framing of this insoluble bond follows form-critical logic and is itself a historical claim. It raises the following question: What is the *Sitz im Leben* of the biblical canon? Multiple *Sitze im Leben* exist within the socioreligious history of the united monarchy, the northern kingdom, and its southern counterpart in the broad and tortuous sweep of Israel's covenantal life before God. These historical and religious causes gave rise to the choir of voices within the Hebrew Scriptures. The canonical approach presented here does not sit uneasily with this religiohistorical phenomenon because an understanding of divine providence does not blush in the face of historical and religious complexity.

In time, however, Israel increasingly identifies itself as a people of the book. Moreover, the canon itself, in Childs's terms, becomes the *Sitz im Leben* for the Jewish community.[12] From this vantage point, the community of faith measures its own existence by the norm of its received canon. The significance of this changing posture toward the traditions of Israel is paramount for an understanding of the canonical approach. A distinction is drawn between the compositional history of biblical books, along with the multiple decisions made along the way to bring the books toward a stable, literary presentation, *and* the reception of those books as normative Scripture in the community of faith. Once

11. Childs, *Introduction*, 78.
12. Childs, *Introduction*, 78.

the tradition-building process or the canonical process of biblical books reaches its final, literary destination, then the understanding of the character of these books as an abiding witness of God's self-revelation and revealed will shapes the community of faith's understanding of the canon's intention. The operating force of divine providence undergirds the entire affair.

The state of affairs described above follows from the biblical texts' own self-understanding. In other words, the recognition of the canon's intention, as a theological understanding of the text's ability, to render God's identity and will for future generations has exegetical warrant. As claimed in a previous chapter, the concept of canon reduced to an external ecclesial decision does not do justice to the "canon consciousness" (*Kanonsbewusstsein*) embedded in the biblical text itself. Texts within the Pentateuch such as Deut. 31:9–13 (on the enduring nature of the law); Exod. 12:4–15 (ritual observance); and Exod. 12:26–27 (transmitting the Passover story) reveal the text's own self-understanding as a normative witness for future generations. The Prophets are replete with such examples (e.g., Isa. 8:16; 30:8; 40:8). The main point drawn from these canonical instincts remains as follows: *the decision to preserve Israel's traditions in written form as a witness for future generations flows from the canon's own self-understanding.* Again, this claim does not deny the multiple historical forces at work that gave rise to the various traditions of Israel. But the collecting, preserving, and shaping of these traditions—whether in the form of law, narrative, prophetic oracle, poetry, or wisdom— received its constraining pressure from an understanding of the canon's enduring character as witness.

Once compositional history elides into textual reception, however fuzzy the line between these two may be, then the situation in Israel's and the church's religious life becomes marked by the anterior authority of their canonical texts. Again, Israel's Scripture *is* the *Sitz im Leben* for synagogue and church. For all the diversity of hermeneutical approaches in the Second Temple period leading up to and during Christianity's infancy—*pesharim* at Qumran, *derash* and *peshat* in protorabbinic and rabbinic sources, *allegory* among Christians, and so forth—one indisputable point holds the variety of hermeneutical approaches together on the formal level: they all understand Israel's Scriptures as a divine word for their current location in time. Such a confession in no way removes the hermeneutical differences between synagogue and synagogue, church and synagogue, and church and church. Nevertheless, this canonical understanding of Israel's Scriptures flows from the biblical text's self-understanding and is, thus, in accord with the canon's intentionality.

The actualization of the Old Testament into new historical situations is part and parcel of canonical intentionality. Readers observe this phenomenon in the Scriptures themselves when, for example, Moses expounds the law on the plains of Moab (Deut. 1:5). The internal tensions that readers of Sacred Scripture feel when working through the Pentateuch's legal code are presented canonically as the application of Mosaic Law to new historical circumstances.[13] Where sacred canon, community of faith, and a confession of faith regarding the continued presence of God among his people come together in combustive force, there, by faith, the canon is operating according to its intended purposes.

All the achievements of historical criticism notwithstanding, a certain amount of collateral damage, intended or not, remains. The relegation of texts to their original historical provenances as phenomena occurring then and there between author/editor(s) and original audience(s) creates significant hurdles for the continued actualization of the text into the current moment.[14] In fact, the

13. See Gerald T. Sheppard, "Canonical Criticism," in *Anchor Bible Dictionary*, ed. D. N. Freedman (New York: Doubleday, 1992), 1:864–65.

14. In his *Tractatus Theologico-Politicus*, Benedict Spinoza clears the space for a hermeneutic of suspicion when he identifies authorial intention historically conceived as the meaning of the text *simpliciter*. He then takes the security of that meaning away by revealing our hermeneutical inability to achieve clarity on this level of inquiry. On this account, meaning-as-origin takes precedence over meaning-as-effect.

canonical process sees to it that the biblical texts may be loosened from their historical particularity for the sake of their divinely governed presence within the community of faith.[15]

For clarity's sake, "loosened" does not mean completely removed from historical particularity. The conceptual dangers here lurk in the generalities. In the editorial process of canonical shaping, some texts' historical particularity is generalized (e.g., Isa. 40–55) while that of other texts is not (e.g., Nahum). Nor does this loosening operate within Gotthold Lessing's philosophical frame where historically particular texts must be deoccasionalized for the sake of their universal truth claims. Moreover, this loosening by no means entails moving beyond the verbal profile of the text in an effort to measure its truth-telling capacity by some external criteria.

Rather, this "loosening from historical particularity" takes seriously the events of the text and their initial reception but does not limit the text's purview or provenance to immediate historical reception. In other words, what this loosening resists is an understanding of the text's events and immediate reception as a totalizing claim on the text's meaning or scope. The community of faith's continued wrestling with its Sacred Scriptures, while seeking to identify God and his will in fresh theological insights and acts of obedience, is most assuredly in the purview of the canonical text as well. Such a claim is a theological judgment about the text's ability to speak into new situations as a divine word, whether the text in the editorial process has been departicularized

15. On Micah, Ehud Ben Zvi makes the following salient point in *Micah*, Forms of Old Testament Literature 21b (Grand Rapids: Eerdmans, 2000), 7:

> It is worth mentioning that no textually inscribed markers indicate that the readership of the book was asked to reread the book or any READING within it in a manner governed by their own awareness of either any proposed redactional history of the book, or by the place of the relevant READINGS in a text other than the present book of Micah, be it a hypothetical forerunner of Micah or any other text. Indeed, it is far more likely that communities of rereaders will continually reread a certain book that they accept as YHWH's word in a way that is governed by the actual text of the book and its textually inscribed demands than by the text of an alternative—and hypothetical—book that they are not reading, rereading, copying, and studying.

or not. I will explore some of these dynamics in chapter 6, on the Trinity and the Old Testament.

The canon therefore anticipates a certain kind of reader. Christopher Seitz quips, "No matter how much the golfer with a sand wedge and cleated shoes wants to play squash, the squash court expects something else: rubber-soled shoes, a squash racket, and a player who has come to play squash."[16] Can a similar claim be made about the canon of Scripture? Does the canon expect its readers to come to it with a set of assumptions and anticipations about the text and the reading process? Can one decision about a reading strategy claim a superior status to others? The canonical approach, in accord with the received reading practices of the church, says yes. When believers read Israel's canon in the anticipation of hearing an authoritative word whose source is the communicative action of God, they read Scripture according to its own intention.[17]

For some readers, the claims of the previous paragraph may seem limiting, if not obscurantist and provincial. From a certain vantage point, these sentiments are understandable. At the same time, moreover, this understanding of canonical intentionality has broad enough shoulders to carry a wide array of interpretive conclusions. It bears repeating: *the canonical approach is a theological framework for reading the Old Testament as Scripture*. It does not flatten the Scriptures into a monotone voice.[18] Neither does it claim that the stability of the canon makes for greener interpretive fields devoid of exegetical sweat, labor, prayer, and sharp disagreement. One only has to take a quick look at the ecclesial

16. Seitz, *Word without End*, 83–84.

17. "The true expositor of the Christian scriptures," Childs reminds, "is the one who awaits in anticipation toward becoming the interpreted rather than the interpreter." Brevard S. Childs, *Biblical Theology of the Old and New Testaments: Theological Reflection on the Christian Bible* (Minneapolis: Fortress, 1992), 86.

18. Speaking of the diverse voices within Scripture, Barth claims, "The distinctions in the content of the witness do not mean a distinction in the witness itself." Karl Barth, *Church Dogmatics*, trans. G. T. Thompson and H. Knight (Edinburgh: T&T Clark, 1956), I/2:482.

landscape of the Western world to recognize very different interpretive conclusions regarding a whole assortment of biblical texts,
doctrinal formulations, and ethical outcomes. Nor is the canonical
approach weighted down with heavy philosophical-hermeneutical
baggage so that unpacking it demands a deconstruction of its
unspoken philosophical commitments, such as claiming that the
canonical approach is New Criticism and, once identified as such,
can be dismissed.

In fact, the canonical approach on the whole is modest in its
hermeneutical claims. It does not overreach or overdetermine exegetical outcomes. The canonical approach recognizes the coercive
pressure of the Word of the Lord to be heard and submitted to in
every generation of the faithful. Again, the community of faith as
the social location of the canonical text cannot be separated from
a proper understanding of what the canon is and intends. This
canonical instinct is not foisted onto the text as a foreign imposition but grows from within the canon's own self-consciousness
and formation. The oft-repeated liturgical formula holds true:
"This *is* the Word of the Lord." And, yes, "thanks be to God."

Canonical Intentionality, Inspiration, and the Holy Spirit

When speaking of the Scripture's intentionality, the canonical
approach sails between a theological Scylla and Charybdis. On
the one hand, the canonical approach affirms the insoluble relationship between text and community, insisting that the former's
proper identification as object is only available from the latter's
perspective and location.[19] In other words, the canon is not an
object that can be detached from its reception by synagogue and
church. On the other hand, the canonical approach maintains a
hard distinction between text and interpreter that keeps the former

---

19. Rowan Williams believes a significant feature of Augustine's legacy is his
theological account of human subjectivity. Christian practice cannot leave time and
body behind. See *On Augustine* (London: Bloomsbury, 2016), ix, chap. 1.

from becoming either a wax nose or a mirror of the interpreter's self. The canonical approach places text above interpreter in full recognition of the text's ability to challenge, falsify, and reform the church and its teaching according to God's revelation.[20] This canonical instinct is similar to Karl Barth's fiddling with the syntax of the third component of biblical exposition, the *usus Scripturae* (use of Scripture). On final analysis, Barth claims, the genitive construction is subjective. The Scriptures make use of us, rather than vice versa.[21]

Theological commitments shape the navigation between these hermeneutical threats. The cliff on the right identifies Scripture as an objective entity existing unto itself apart from the community of faith. The cliff on the left understands Scripture as the wish projection of various interpretive communities inescapably sullied by interpretive bias. Navigating between these two perilous interpretive cliffs is not first and foremost the product of philosophical or hermeneutical categories, as helpful as these may be when deployed in responsible ways. Safe passage is granted by a robust commitment to the operative agency of God with his Scriptures by means of the Holy Spirit. "The Christian doctrine of the role of the Holy Spirit is not a hermeneutical principle," Childs claims, "but that divine reality itself who makes understanding of God possible."[22]

From one angle, the history of interpretation highlights the gulf between text and interpreter. Interpreters can never completely escape the changing historical and cultural forces at work around them. A fair understanding of *sola Scriptura* affirms this dynamic, as the Scriptures themselves are deemed authoritative for matters of

20. The claim here is about the theological ordering of Scripture and tradition in relation to each other. It is by no means a dismissal of tradition, because Scripture and tradition are inseparable. It is worth recalling that Reformation debates over the claims of Scripture vis-à-vis the Roman Catholic magisterium were equally debates about who has the better claim on the church fathers.
21. Barth, *Church Dogmatics*, I/2:738.
22. Childs, *Biblical Theology*, 87.

doctrine and practice, while keeping the interpretation of Scripture a related but distinct doctrinal matter. *Sola Scriptura* is not *sola Hermeneia*.[23] While this distinction and the hermeneutical problems highlighted in literary-critical discussion of the current day may lead some to relativistic conclusions, this need not be the case. A theological account of this problem stresses the ongoing activity of exegesis in the life of the church and a "profounder grasp of the dynamic function of the Bible as the vehicle of an ever fresh word of God to each generation."[24] In other words, the hermeneutical problem is, on final analysis, not a closed door but a wide-open gate. This open gate is cause for interpretive joy and anticipation because of a confession that God by his Spirit is the operative agent of his own Word as it breaks forth on his people in each new generation.[25]

An illustration may serve the point here. In Charles Marsh's recent biography of Dietrich Bonhoeffer, Marsh highlights the role Scripture plays in Bonhoeffer's wrestling with his theological and pastoral vocation.[26] More particularly, the Sermon on the Mount ascended to the top of the heap as Bonhoeffer struggled to overcome the negative effects of a misinformed two-kingdoms theology, by which Christians passively or actively embraced National Socialism because it was an earthly kingdom matter, separate from the

23. It should be added that *sola Scriptura* is not *nuda Scriptura*. It is misguided to have a "no creed but Jesus" understanding of *sola Scriptura*, where Scripture's proper interpretive context is removed from the social location of the church militant and triumphant. The Cartesian dismissal of the presumptive authority of the past would smell like strange soup to the magisterial Reformers and their immediate progeny. See Michael Allen and Scott R. Swain, *Reformed Catholicity: The Promise of Retrieval for Theology and Biblical Interpretation* (Grand Rapids: Baker Academic, 2015).

24. Childs, *Biblical Theology*, 88.

25. For further delving into agency of the Holy Spirit in Christian reading practices, see John Webster, *The Domain of the Word: Scripture and Theological Reason* (London: T&T Clark, 2012), chap. 3. Webster makes a helpful distinction between "illuminated" reading and "pneumatic" reading. The latter suspends the natural properties of texts and readers, while the former does not (62).

26. Charles Marsh, *Strange Glory: A Life of Dietrich Bonhoeffer* (New York: Knopf, 2014), 149, 217, 243. Compare this view with Bonhoeffer's earlier understanding of the nonapplicability of the Sermon on the Mount to modern Christians (Marsh, *Strange Glory*, 85).

concerns of God's kingdom. Bonhoeffer, even in contradistinction from Barth, recognized that Scripture will not allow theology a "wholly other" status and demands its embodiment in the real *Sturm und Drang* (storm and stress) of human existence. The Sermon on the Mount served Bonhoeffer's theological and political wrestling in profound ways. The result was his celebrated work *The Cost of Discipleship (Nachfolge)*.[27]

Does this mean that Bonhoeffer's reading of the Sermon on the Mount is the final word? By no means. In fact, recent work on the Sermon on the Mount takes umbrage with Bonhoeffer at several points. Or put more positively, recent research on the Sermon highlights aspects that Bonhoeffer was either unaware of, did not see, or dismissed. Also, whole hermeneutical families might raise serious questions about the applicability of the Sermon on the Mount to Christian practice. We have no need to sort through these interpretive matters here, but the simple point remains. In a critical moment in Bonhoeffer's wrestling with the implications of the gospel for the German church, the Sermon on the Mount in its given literary form had a graciously tyrannical influence on Bonhoeffer's formulations. Similar claims pertain to the book of Romans at key junctures in the church's interpretive tradition, as with Augustine, Luther, and Barth.

The glory of the Christian canon is its ability to do this kind of work continually in the life of Christ's church, requiring a robust doctrine of the Holy Spirit to fuel its fire. The reader may sense a hesitation to label this hermeneutical strategy with the familiar terms of philosophical hermeneutics. This hesitation does not come from a lack of appreciation for philosophical hermeneutics and what it might offer. Nevertheless, philosophical hermeneutics does not have the necessary tools to identify the particular issues at stake in this account of canon and intentionality.[28] For the

---

27. Dietrich Bonhoeffer, *The Cost of Discipleship*, rev. ed. (New York: Macmillan, 1972). Original German edition: *Nachfolge* (Munich: Kaiser, 1937).

28. See Stephen E. Fowl's helpful articulation of the theological issues that arise when philosophical hermeneutics is applied to theological interpretation. Especially

means by which these interpretive seas are navigated, even with all the important sailing accoutrements on board, is the rudder of God's Spirit. The gap between text and interpreter is not bridged by more refined hermeneutical tools, helpful as these may be. The gap is bridged by a Person.

Conclusion

John Webster is right to claim, "Whether done well or ill, theology and the study of Scripture are spiritual tasks, and the conditions for their flourishing include spiritual conditions."[29] The spiritual conditions needed for the task of reading Scripture are concomitant with the spiritual conditions for coming to terms with the canon's intentionality. Such a confession does not provide a green light for interpreters to leave behind the creaturely character of Scripture and its verbal form. On this account, the text of Scripture and its verbal profile provide a jumping point for the interpreter to exercise theological imagination two or three steps removed from Scripture itself. Rather, the recognition of the spiritual nature of the task places all the tools of critical inquiry into Scripture's verbal form, at the foot of the canon's overwhelming intention: to hear the word of the Lord.

---

helpful is his engagement with the interpretive legacy of J. L. Austin's speech-act theory as presented in Austin's *How to Do Things with Words: The William James Lectures Delivered at Harvard University in 1955*, ed. J. O. Urmson and Marina Sbisà, 2nd ed. (Cambridge, MA: Harvard University Press, 1975). Identifying himself in the Richard Rorty and Jeffrey Stout stream of Austin reception over against the John Searle, Anthony Thiselton, and Kevin Vanhoozer stream, Fowl is less than happy about speech-act theory's utility in securing authorial intentionality for theological interpretation. Stephen E. Fowl, *Theological Interpretation of Scripture* (Eugene, OR: Cascade Books, 2009), 37–53, esp. 47–50.

29. Webster, *Domain of the Word*, 4.

4

Canon and Textual Criticism

The Search for the Christian Bible

The previous chapters place a high premium on the final form of the biblical books. The object of exegetical and theological inquiry is the biblical book itself as a literary whole. The previous chapters also defined intentionality as a textual phenomenon of the Holy Spirit's teaching office. In other words, intentionality is not uncovered primarily by moving backward to human agents and social settings but by prioritizing divine authorship as the defining property of Scripture's continued existence. Yet a basic question follows from these claims: What text(s) are we talking about? On the surface of things, this question is fair and straightforward. We are talking about Isaiah as a sixty-six-chapter whole or Jeremiah's fifty-two chapters, complex as Jeremiah's literary structure is. Still, a lingering question persists about how readers establish Isaiah's or Jeremiah's final form as a material object. These kinds of basic and material questions reside within the world of textual criticism and its continued service to biblical studies. A few introductory comments may aid in contextualizing textual criticism's important role.

If there was ever a time when the Old Testament text was understood as a simple phenomenon whose literary origins can be easily traced and identified, such a day no longer exists. Given today's textual evidence, it seems Pollyannaish to hope for a clear and tidy picture of the Old Testament literary tree moving from its oral/literary roots to mature textual form. The reconstruction of the biblical text's literary history remains the stuff of critical inquiry nowhere near consensus. Why? Because if critical Old Testament scholarship assures us of anything, it is that the textual situation in the Second Temple period was pluriform, lacking the kind of uniformity a "religion of the book" needs to sustain itself.

Moreover, the text's prehistory and posthistory are complex, as attested in the various forms of the biblical books on offer in the textual evidence. Textual reconstruction, or establishing the text itself—the task traditionally ascribed to textual criticism— necessitates carefully sifting through the Hebrew textual traditions and the early translations, such as the Septuagint.[1] Given the plethora of evidence, text-critical work is no simple task. And while the canonical approach affirms a theological priority for the final literary form of the biblical texts, it does so with the

---

1. The goal of textual criticism remains a matter of some dispute among scholars. Paul de Lagarde and Paul Kahle represent the two approaches that stand as models, despite significant differences in text-critical execution. For Lagarde, the goal is establishing the *Urtext* (original text) by deploying various text-critical tools. The assumption underlying Lagarde's goal is that textual differences can best be explained by a linear, genetic account where the *Urtext*, or original literary form, underwent various changes/corruptions that need to be sorted out to establish the original form. Kahle, on the other hand, posited the very opposite of Lagarde's approach. For Kahle, there is no uniform *Urtext* but instead multiple pristine texts whose differences are best explained by various geographical locations. My sympathies are with Lagarde, although I recognize the complexity attendant to any account of the literary history of biblical books, especially given that some stages of a book's literary development were accepted as authoritative at that time, even though the book had not reached its final literary stabilization (Jeremiah is a case in point). For a nuanced and helpful argument for the *Urtext* thesis, see Emanuel Tov, "Post-Modern Textual Criticism?," in *Greek Scriptures and the Rabbis*, ed. T. M. Law and A. Salvesen (Leuven: Peeters, 2012), 1–18.

knowledge that such a commitment does not abdicate the necessity of continued textual criticism or establishing of the final literary form itself.

This chapter does not pretend to offer a full presentation of textual criticism and the various tools needed for this work. Several good works on the subject exist, and that wheel does not need to be re-created here.[2] Rather, what this chapter seeks to offer is a set of theological instincts that can help us navigate the stormy and overwhelming sea of textual evidence. No evidence is self-interpreting, whether textual or archaeological. And while it may seem counterintuitive to speak of the canonical implications of Holy Scripture in a situation of textual pluriformity, this chapter will argue the opposite. Textual pluriformity and Holy Scripture's canonical status are not at odds with one another, whether in our day or in the early days of Jesus and the apostles. Also, and crucially, this chapter will make the case for the coexistence of a pluriform and uniform textual tradition in the first-century world of the apostles rather than reinforcing the popular line that textual pluriformity led to uniformity in a historically linear mode of development. Let's move to clarifying what these terms and claims are all about.

Texts, Texts, and More Texts: Pluriformity, Uniformity, and Multiple Canons

The discovery of the Dead Sea Scrolls put the fox among the hens of earlier textual theories. The earlier theories were straightforward and were presented as follows: Most ancient translations, such as the Septuagint (LXX), resignified the Hebrew text for its readers, in this case a Greek-speaking audience. Where the

2. Emanuel Tov, *Textual Criticism of the Hebrew Bible*, 3rd ed. (Minneapolis: Fortress, 2012); Ernst Würthwein, *The Text of the Old Testament: An Introduction to the "Biblia Hebraica,"* ed. A. A. Fischer, trans. E. F. Rhodes, 3rd ed. (Grand Rapids: Eerdmans, 2014).

Septuagint goes its own way vis-à-vis the Hebrew text, then the translator's own idiosyncratic translating tendencies or theological instincts are on display. These departures, however, were of little to no value for textual criticism, that is, the establishment of the final form of the proto-Masoretic tradition.[3] Put in other terms, the idiosyncratic character of the LXX at various places provides no evidence for differing *Vorlagen*, or background Hebrew texts, which are needed at the table of text-critical evidence. So went the older theory. Text-critical life was simpler in those days, but that was then.

The Dead Sea Scrolls caused the older textual theories to list to the starboard bow, ultimately capsizing in full. Why? Because some of the Hebrew biblical scrolls found in the caves at Qumran overlapped with the "idiosyncratic" readings of the Septuagintal translators. The result of this discovery changed the face of modern textual criticism. Now the Septuagint, once marginalized in text-critical studies, is seen as providing possible access to Hebrew *Vorlagen* (background texts) once sealed away.[4]

3. The MT, the Masoretic Text, is the technical term for the Hebrew text that serves as the basis for most critical editions of the Hebrew Bible. In this sense, the Hebrew Bible, unlike the critical editions of the New Testament, operates with a Textus Receptus, a received text. The Leningrad Codex (L) provides the textual stability for the MT because it is the best "complete" manuscript of this scribal tradition. *The Hebrew University Bible* bases its MT form on a diplomatic edition of the Aleppo Codex, an incomplete manuscript though its extant parts are the best of the Masoretic codices. On the other hand, *The Oxford Hebrew Bible* aims at a comprehensive critical edition. This edition takes the broader evidence into account in the textual production of the Hebrew Bible itself.

4. Emanuel Tov provides a helpful handle for how to wade through these complexities. One, if the LXX text exhibits the tendency to paraphrase throughout the book, then the text is an unstable source for reconstructing an alternative textual *Vorlage*. If, on the other hand, the book on offer demonstrates a tendency to more literal translations, with minimal paraphrasing, then the text provides a possible avenue for alternative textual reconstruction. Tov understands Septuagintal translators as consistent in their translation method throughout their respective books. See "The Septuagint as a Source for the Literary Analysis of Hebrew Scripture," in *Exploring the Origins of the Bible: Canon Formation in Historical, Literary, and Theological Perspective*, ed. C. A. Evans and E. Tov (Grand Rapids: Baker Academic, 2008), 33.

One of the more widely known examples is Jeremiah in the LXX and MT. The differences between these two texts are marked, with the former almost half the size of the latter. Traditional theories suggested that the LXX version of Jeremiah is a whittled-down form of its parent text for the sake of a Gentile readership. A Hebrew fragment of Jeremiah from Cave 4 at Qumran suggests otherwise. Although the surviving text is only fragmentary, it overlaps with LXX Jeremiah in its differences from the Masoretic tradition at key points. This finding provides empirical evidence that counters the traditional understanding of LXX Jeremiah's relationship to the Hebrew text. LXX Jeremiah is no longer best understood as a resignified text. It is a translation of a Hebrew text of Jeremiah that is different from and shorter than the one presented in the Masoretic tradition. It is unclear what to make of this evidence; no evidence is self-interpreting. Nevertheless, we cannot quickly dismiss Emanuel Tov's suggestion that LXX Jeremiah provides evidence of a biblical book in the midst of its own literary history.

As the previous paragraphs intimate, these findings at Qumran and the Septuagint's renewed place at the table of evidence reveal a scene of textual pluriformity during the second century BC and onward into the first century of the Christian era. These findings problematize the notion of canon, especially if canon is conceived of as a formalized list. To speak of a canon during this period, therefore, seems absurd at first glance. Critics of the canonical approach often fire a quick shot from their holster: What canon are we talking about?

The religious and historical argument goes something like this: the Qumran documents and the LXX leave little doubt as to the textual situation on the ground during the Second Temple period; the textual tradition of the Hebrew Scriptures was pluriform. How and why the uniform tradition preserved by the Masoretes displaced this earlier textual pluriformity has been the subject of critical inquiry for some time. The *how* is still a matter of some dispute.[5] The *why* relates to the ascendency of Pharisaic Judaism after AD 70 and the exigencies of religious life after the destruction of the temple. Pharisaic Judaism as a religious group survived the destruction of the temple, while other expressions of Judaism died out. The displacement of a pluriform textual tradition with a uniform one results from a historical accident: a particular religious class won the day. And to the winner go the spoils, or in this case, their canon.

The above description contains matters of scholarly dispute, but sorting through them here would unnecessarily distract us from the goal of this chapter. Still, the canonical history rehearsed above understands, and quite reasonably so, the literary history as a linear one moving from pluriformity to uniformity. A pluriform canon in time yields to a uniform, stable textual tradition: a tradition preserved by the Masoretic scribal guild.

Given the known evidence, another possibility exists. Instead of uniformity displacing pluriformity in time, the one eliding into the other, perhaps a pluriform textual tradition and a uniform one coexisted on parallel historical tracks. Adam S. van der Woude makes a strong argument for this second understanding, an argument that this author finds persuasive.[6] Van der Woude believes that the textual findings at Masada, Wadi Murabbaʿat, and Naḥal Ḥever provide another angle of evidence. On van der Woude's account, the reality of a uniform textual tradition among the gatekeepers of rabbinic Judaism in AD 70 and beyond suggests the presence of a uniform textual tradition before

5. The notion of a council at Jamnia in AD 90 where the rabbinic canon was determined is no longer a sound theory. There is no evidence that canonical decisions were made at this council. See Jack P. Lewis, "Jamnia Revisited," in *The Canon Debate*, ed. L. M. McDonald and J. A. Sanders (Peabody, MA: Hendrickson, 2002), 146–62.

6. Adam S. van der Woude, "Pluriformity and Uniformity: Reflections on the Transmission of the Old Testament," in *Sacred History and Sacred Text in Early Judaism: A Symposium in Honour of A. S. van der Woude*, ed. J. N. Bremmer and F. García Martínez (Kampen: Kok Pharos, 1992), 151–69.

TEXTUAL PLURIFORMITY/UNIFORMITY: The plethora of text and text types discovered in the twentieth century complicates the text-critical pursuit of an "original" Old Testament text. A standard view of the Old Testament's textual history is that a pluriform text type—multiple and divergent texts and text types—in time yielded to a uniform text associated with rabbinic Judaism of the era after AD 70. This chapter makes a different claim: uniformity and pluriformity existed on parallel historical tracks, rather than pluriformity leading genetically into uniformity.

this time.[7] There is evidence from the Judean Desert to support this.

A Greek translation of the Minor Prophets found at Naḥal Ḥever dates to the latter part of the second century BC. Remarkably, this Minor Prophets scroll is a revision of the Septuagint tradition based on a Hebrew text that is similar to the proto-Masoretic tradition. Later first- and second-century AD revisions (recensions) of the LXX tradition toward a proto-Masoretic background text are no novelty within the history of the Greek translation tradition, as shown by the work of Aquila, Symmachus, and Theodotion.[8] Rather, evidence from the second century BC leans in another direction. Already, in certain circles, Septuagintal forms based on a different Hebrew background text (non-proto-Masoretic) or texts deemed too paraphrastic in nature were brought into stricter conformity with the proto-Masoretic tradition. In other words, van der Woude believes the historical

7. Masada is the famed mountain fortress in the desert of Judea, where the last resistors of Roman occupation remained until their sacrificial end in AD 73. Fragments of Genesis, Leviticus, Deuteronomy, Ezekiel, and the Psalms were discovered at Masada dating to this time. All these fragments are proto-Masoretic in form. During the Bar Kokhba revolt (132–35), Jewish resistance fighters hid themselves in inaccessible areas of the Judean Desert. At Wadi Murabbaʿat, one of these regions of the Bar Kokhba revolt, biblical manuscripts were discovered as well, all proto-Masoretic in form.

8. These three provided new translations of the Hebrew text into Greek during the second and third centuries AD, Theodotion with the help of an existing Greek text.

accidents leading to the ascendency and preservation of rabbinic Judaism, along with their textual tradition, had antecedents before AD 70.[9] Though the evidence is not conclusive, the temple cult, its liturgy, and the scribal culture provide a fitting, if not compelling, sociological and religious context for a uniform textual tradition before this time.[10]

9. Based on the evidence at Masada and Wadi Murabbaʿat, Tov suggests the "master copies" of these proto-Masoretic forms discovered in the Judean Desert are associated with the temple. Emanuel Tov, "The Text of the Hebrew/Aramaic and Greek Bible Used in the Ancient Synagogue," in *Hebrew Bible, Greek Bible, and Qumran* (Tübingen: Mohr Siebeck, 2008), 177. Tov also emphasizes that all the discoveries in the Judean Desert are of the proto-Masoretic textual family except for the findings at Qumran. Tov's classification of the Qumran texts has gained broad acceptance. Rather than identifying texts geographically—Babylon (MT), Alexandria (LXX), Palestine (SP = Samaritan Pentateuch)—Tov identifies them by their literary and textual character traits: MT-like texts; pre-Samaritan texts; texts close to Hebrew source of LXX; and non-aligned texts. Tov, *Textual Criticism of the Hebrew Bible*, 108–9. The MT-like texts dominate the landscape, even at Qumran. Tov believes the findings in the Judean Desert outside of Qumran, most likely texts indicative of those used in synagogue worship in the first century AD, witness to the normativity of the MT-like or proto-Masoretic textual tradition. He clarifies, "As far as we know, none of these groups of texts had a close connection to the texts used in the synagogue. Nor did the Hebrew *Vorlage* of the LXX derive from temple circles" ("Ancient Synagogue," 175). The slight differences between the MT-like texts at Qumran and the other MT-like texts in the Judean Desert (e.g., Masada) indicate two types of Masoretic scrolls: an inner circle of protorabbinic scrolls that agree with the medieval Masoretic Text and a second circle of scrolls that are very similar to it. The inner-circle texts and their broad textual agreement make the theory of a "master copy" located in the temple a strong possibility (177–78).

10. The temple cult and its library are not sufficient causes for canonization proper, but they are *necessary* causes. In other words, it may be beyond the available evidence to identify the temple library as a protocanonical repository. At the same time, books "canonized" in time were in the temple library. For example, Ben Sira was most likely in the temple library but is not a part of the Masoretic canon. Framing the matter well is Karel van der Toorn, *Scribal Culture and the Making of the Hebrew Bible* (Cambridge, MA: Harvard University Press, 2007), 244:

> Though the presence of a text in a library need not imply canonicity, it does mean that the text in question had entered the stream of tradition. Libraries embodied the literary and scholarly heritage. And a work had to be perceived as "traditional"—or "ancestral" (*patrōios*), as the Prologue of Ben Sira has it—as a precondition for becoming canonical. In this sense, inclusion in the library was a condition for inclusion in the canon; however, inclusion in the library was a not a ticket to canonization.

If, then, the findings at Masada intimate a master copy at the temple, then the textual discrimination toward the proto-Masoretic Text form has taken place in the

This subject ranks as one of the more complex fields of inquiry in Old Testament scholarship. Lack of evidence and diversity of opinion about the scant evidence make for turbulent waters. Given the pluriformity of the textual traditions at Qumran, one is hard-pressed to make a case for a standardized or stabilized biblical text across the broad stream of the Second Temple period. At the same time, the evidence from outside Qumran leans in the direction of a uniform textual tradition on a parallel track with the pluriform biblical texts. As mentioned in the previous paragraph, the gravitational force of the temple cult with its liturgy and scribal guild provides a possible avenue for understanding one of these quarters and its organic relationship with rabbinic Judaism after AD 70.

Our attention will return to this matter toward the end of this chapter, but it is worth pointing out the theological significance of Jesus's encounters and debates with early Judaism. Differences abound in spades between these interlocutors when it comes to interpretation. Nevertheless, Jesus and the Pharisees, for example, do not debate the character and scope of their scriptural heritage, despite open-ended questions about canonical fixity during this period.[11] There appears to be a shared, common body of Scriptures, and this sharing appears linked with the temple and its cult. Moreover, this sharing is of some theological import for the Christian reception of the Hebrew Scriptures and applies some pressure on the decision to prioritize the Hebrew text over its Greek translation, the Septuagint. Our attention now turns to this juggernaut of an issue.

---

temple scribal culture roughly during the same period of textual pluriformity one discovers at Qumran (see note above).

11. "It would appear," Gallagher and Meade conclude, "that in the era before canon lists, there was a 'limited set of books that was a functional collection of authoritative texts' on which all or most Jews could agree." Edmon L. Gallagher and John D. Meade, *The Biblical Canon Lists from Early Christianity: Text and Analysis* (Oxford: Oxford University Press, 2017), 25. See also Stephen Chapman, *The Law and the Prophets*, Forschungen zum Alten Testament 27 (Tübingen: Mohr Siebeck, 2000), 266–68. Gallagher and Meade recognize that the so-called Sadducean canon as a Torah-only canon is a matter of dispute. Patristic references in this direction are dubitable (*Biblical Canon Lists*, 19–20).

Which Canon: The Hebrew Text, the Septuagint, or Both?

Students who are new to the subject matter are often surprised to discover that the MT as a text dates to around AD 900–1000. The overlap of this medieval manuscript tradition with the proto-Masoretic Text discussed in the section above is a staggering achievement of preservation. Nevertheless, until the discovery of the Dead Sea Scrolls, our best witnesses to the Hebrew text tradition were medieval sources.

The Greek translation of the Hebrew text—the Septuagint, or LXX—presents its own text-critical challenges, but as mentioned above, it remains indispensable as a text-critical source. The Septuagint also presents another challenge to the Christian church, especially related to the challenge of biblical-theological reflection and articulation. Given the enormous influence of the LXX on the New Testament's own compositional history and early Christian engagement with the Old Testament, should we prioritize the Hebrew text, or should the Septuagint have pride of place canonically? This straightforward question resists a straightforward answer. The Christian church universal has been divided on this matter since the sixteenth century. We will attempt to sort through some of the complex challenges, yet the reader should be forewarned: a final solution to this problem is not waiting at the end of this chapter.

We must first state clearly that there is no such thing as *the* Septuagint. In other words, the term "Septuagint," or "LXX" (the seventy), refers to the tradition of Old Greek translators from Alexandria, Egypt, in the third century BC, who first set out to translate their Hebrew Scriptures into Greek. The scribes in Alexandria did not invent the act or art of translation. Nevertheless, this particular act of translation was the first of its kind in the Western world: a religious text of generous scope whose genesis rests in the mouth of God.[12] Our access to the Old Greek

---

12. Tessa Rajak, *Translation and Survival: The Greek Bible of the Jewish Diaspora* (Oxford: Oxford University Press, 2009). See also Timothy Michael Law, *When God*

of these second-century translators bogs down under the text-critical enterprise of the LXX itself. Layer upon layer of additions or corrections (recensions) to the Old Greek are stored in later manuscripts housing the LXX. At times, establishing the Old Greek translations is itself a complex matter of text-critical discernment. Our critical editions of the LXX are exactly that: critical editions coming to terms with vast amounts of textual evidence for the LXX (Old Greek) and later recensional activity. As we observed from van der Woude in the section above, the modifying of Greek translations to be in closer proximity to the proto-Masoretic Text took place before the first century AD and was not simply the activity of the later Aquila, Symmachus, and Theodotion in reaction to the Christian reception of the LXX.[13]

Matters pertaining to the study of the Septuagint are thorny; this should come as no surprise, since most critical issues are. At the same time, the field of Septuagintal study is one of the more interesting and productive areas of biblical research today.[14] Though a detailed examination of these Septuagint studies exceeds the parameters of this book, it will suffice to affirm the following: by the first century of the Christian era, the Hebrew Scriptures and a range of other books often referred to as deuterocanonical were available in Greek translation.

Spoke Greek: The Septuagint and the Making of the Christian Bible (Oxford: Oxford University Press, 2013), 34–35.

13. The notion that Aquila's translation in the second century AD was generated from anti-Christian concerns remains a contested matter. Abraham Wasserstein and David J. Wasserstein claim, "But no source from the tannaitic period suggests that the translation of Aquila was made for the purpose of counteracting the Christian use made of the LXX." *The Legend of the Septuagint: From Classical Antiquity to Today* (Cambridge: Cambridge University Press, 2006), 62. These authors draw the following conclusions: (1) Aquila translated the by-then canonized Hebrew text literally, word for word; (2) this text remained closely allied with the traditional exegesis of the rabbis (62).

14. The list of LXX scholars is growing, but I draw your attention to the work of Kristin De Troyer, Arie van der Kooij, Ross Wagner, Emanuel Tov, Michael Law, Jan Joosten, and Martin Hengel, to name a few.

As one might argue on analogy to the influence of the King James Version on the English language, the Greek translations of the Old Testament played a formative role in accessing, hearing, and understanding the Old Testament in a Greek-speaking culture.[15] For simplicity's sake, we refer to these Greek translations as the LXX, but remember that there is no such thing as *the* LXX. Whenever a critical edition of the Septuagint is handled (e.g., Rahlfs-Hanhart), van der Toorn's sagacious reminder should be at the forefront of our memory: "The broader selection of the Septuagint has at times been taken to imply that the Jews at Alexandria, where the translation originated, had a larger canon than the Palestinian Jews. The discussion is somewhat spurious, because the term 'canon' is inappropriate in this context. There was no Septuagint as yet, only Greek translations and adaptations of various Hebrew books; the Greek Bible is an invention of a later time."[16] Van der Toorn's framing of the issues clarifies the distinction between matters that might understandably be confused.

But What about the LXX and Early Christianity?

The historical accident of the LXX's influence on the compositional history of the New Testament and early Christian biblical interpretation raises a pressing question. Why do Protestants use the Hebrew text as the basis for their translations and not the LXX? As mentioned, this is a thorny problem whose solution resists easy answers. A few matters need to be sorted out.

15. Gordon Campbell compares the LXX and the King James Bible in terms of the expansive collaborative work by the various translators. In Campbell's understanding of this comparison, the King James Bible is the first of its kind since the Old Greek translation of the Hebrew Scriptures. *Bible: The Story of the King James Version, 1611–2011* (Oxford: Oxford University Press, 2010), 39–40. Given the broad use of the KJV in the English-speaking world, it should come as no surprise that, like the LXX, some who had such high value for the text began to argue for the inspiration of its translators (147).

16. Van der Toorn, *Scribal Culture*, 262.

First, the New Testament use of the Old Testament bears a striking resemblance to Tov's textual taxonomy for the Dead Sea Scrolls. As already mentioned, Tov describes the texts at Qumran according to their families: MT-like, Hebrew text similar to LXX, Proto-Samaritan, and Non-Aligned. Besides the Proto-Samaritan text types, the New Testament citations follow a similar pattern. For the most part, the New Testament quotes texts that correspond to the LXX, but most of these LXX-like quotations overlap closely enough with the MT that the distinction is negligible. In other words, nothing of the text's sense is lost by appeal to the MT or the LXX because the latter faithfully adheres to the former on the linguistic and conceptual level. At certain points the New Testament quotation goes the way of the LXX over against the MT where the two diverge on the linguistic and conceptual level. And at other points the quotation mirrors the MT over the LXX, with some quotations remaining nonaligned.[17] These nonaligned texts are due to numerous factors: citations from memory, translations on the go, or differing Greek manuscripts are all possibilities.

To claim that the LXX was the only version of the Old Testament that the New Testament writers used overly simplifies a complex textual witness, despite the incontrovertible presence of the LXX across large swaths of the NT canon.[18] Some scholarly care is called for in this context. For example, David Sapp makes a case for Paul's allusion to Isa. 53 as necessarily MT-like over against the LXX because the MT provides the theological point

17. Jobes and Silva refer to a study by D. M. Turpie in the nineteenth century from which, on the basis of 275 NT passages, the following statistics were drawn: the NT, LXX, and Hebrew text "agree in only about 20 percent of the quotations. Of the 80 percent where some disagreement occurs, less than 5 percent agree with the Hebrew against the LXX, while about a third of the quotations agree with the LXX against the Hebrew." The remaining quotations agree with neither the Hebrew nor the LXX, reflecting paraphrase or various Greek MSS. Karen H. Jobes and Moisés Silva, *Invitation to the Septuagint*, 2nd ed. (Grand Rapids: Baker Academic, 2015), 207.

18. Lim makes a similar claim, "It is an oversimplification to say that the Septuagint was Paul's Bible." Timothy H. Lim, *The Formation of the Jewish Canon*, Anchor Yale Bible Reference Library (New Haven: Yale University Press, 2013), 176.

that Paul is after while the LXX mutes it. His conclusion is worth reproducing in full: "The Greek version of Isaiah 53 offers the Christian exegete considerably less support than the Hebrew versions of the doctrine of the atonement from sin through Jesus' sacrificial death and resurrection."[19] Sapp continues, "We cannot, therefore, expect to find allusions to Isaiah 53:9a or 10–11b in the New Testament in support of the Christian gospel by looking to the LXX. Only the Hebrew texts preserve the language and theology that would make such allusions possible."[20] To be fair, Sapp's arguments about the necessity of the Hebrew text for allusions to Isa. 53 can in other instances be utilized in a different direction.[21]

Identifying the heavy presence of the LXX in the New Testament is one thing. Coming to terms with the enduring theological and practical significance of this indubitable verity is another. Sorting through New Testament quotations of the Old by quantitative analysis—identifying the heavier percentage of the LXX in the New Testament over against the Hebrew text—misses the larger point. Or perhaps to put it better, such analysis is not self-interpreting. An important hermeneutical matter needs to be kept before us when sorting through this material and coming to terms with the continued significance of the LXX. The New Testament authors could make use of an LXX form of the text as a proper extrapolation or interpretation or resignification of the Hebrew text, but

19. David A. Sapp, "The LXX, 1QIsa, and MT Versions of Isaiah 53 and the Christian Doctrine of the Atonement," in *Jesus and the Suffering Servant: Isaiah 53 and Christian Origins*, ed. W. H. Bellinger and W. R. Farmer (Harrisburg, PA: Trinity Press International, 1998), 186.

20. Sapp, "LXX, 1QIsa, and MT," 187.

21. See the examples in Law, *When God Spoke Greek*, chap. 9. Some of Law's examples may be contested, e.g., Isa. 61 in Luke 4. Law's claim that "recovering sight to the blind is nowhere in the Hebrew version of Isaiah 61:1 and instead comes as a direct citation from the Septuagint" (102) does not do justice to the lexical and text-critical matters at play in this verse. Indeed, given various lexical and text-critical data, "recovering sight to the blind" is a fair understanding of the Hebrew of Isa. 61:1 (פקח), a point that Law does not address in his argument. See Mark S. Gignilliat, "God Speaks Hebrew: The Hebrew Text and Septuagint in the Search for the Christian Bible," *Pro Ecclesia* 25 (2016): 154–72.

such instances necessitate neither (1) unfamiliarity with the Hebrew text nor (2) a preference for the Greek vis-à-vis the Hebrew.[22] Rather, on analogy to exegetical practices at Qumran as well as early rabbinic exegesis, the Jewish Christian exegete had an array of exegetical tools that allowed the LXX to function as a legitimate understanding or application of the Hebrew text.[23]

Speaking about rabbinic exegesis, Abraham Wasserstein and David Wasserstein clarify this hermeneutical freedom well: "We have no reason to be surprised that these Rabbis, sometimes alleged to be blindly devoted to the deadening letter of the Law, had the freedom to interpret freely according to the need of the moment both the Hebrew original and the Greek translation which could not in any case be seen as anything more than an interpretation, an exegetical exercise, a kind of commentary, on Holy Writ."[24] On analogy, a similar claim may be brought forward with

22. The New Testament authors do not demonstrate a concern for textual precision in their quotations, as Michael Graves points out. *The Inspiration and Interpretation of Scripture: What the Early Church Can Teach Us* (Grand Rapids: Eerdmans, 2014), 100. On the Letter of Aristeas's history of reception, see Wasserstein and Wasserstein, *Legend*.

23. These exegetical or reading strategies include *ketiv*, "[what is] written," versus *qere*, "[what is to be] read"; and scribal use of *'al tiqre'*, "alternative readings." See Tov, *Textual Criticism of the Hebrew Bible*, for explication of these practices. Bauckham's conclusion regarding the Amos 9:12 LXX quote in Acts 15:16 bears repeating. "Thus there is not the slightest difficulty in supposing that a Jewish Christian exegete, familiar with the Hebrew text of the Bible but writing in Greek, should have welcomed the exegetical potential of the LXX text of Amos 9:12 as a legitimate way of reading the Hebrew text of that verse." Richard Bauckham, "James and the Jerusalem Church," in *The Book of Acts in Its Palestinian Setting*, ed. R. Bauckham (Grand Rapids: Eerdmans, 1995), 456.

24. Wasserstein and Wasserstein, *Legend*, 86; on 85 they further claim:

In any case, the rabbinic transmission of many scriptural passages in respect of which, on occasion, we are seemingly advised not to read what we find in our Hebrew Bible but some other reading (*al tiqre*) surely does not mean that the Rabbis in those passages were engaging in what we should now call emendation in the exercise of textual criticism. On the contrary, while closely adhering to the transmitted text they were, in such cases (of *al tiqre*), allowing themselves the exercise of their freedom and of their imagination in order to see and extract from Scripture all that they knew was lying there to be discovered, including such meanings as could be extracted from the text only by momentarily reading something slightly different from what one ordinarily read there. A

regard to the New Testament authors. They also demonstrate an exegetical freedom where the text's theological potential broadens to include the readings provided by the Septuagintal translators. In doing so, however, they are not involved in text-critical activities as practiced today. Instead, they are demonstrating a more basic theological issue (and problem): the distinction between scriptural normativity and the fixity of language. Lexical potential for New Testament authors is less circumscribed than what is typical of modern lexical practice.

To put the matter another way, the overwhelming evidence for the LXX in the New Testament does not necessitate its priority over the Hebrew *Vorlage*. It reveals an understanding of the translated text as a theological resource for making theological sense in a Greek-speaking world. Moreover, and this point cannot be emphasized enough, the Gospel writers and Paul shared the canonical instincts of Pharisaic Judaism, the progenitor of the Masoretic Text. Points of dispute on the hermeneutical level abound. Nevertheless, the Pharisaic canon, or perhaps the canon associated with the temple, provides a common starting point for these interpretive differences, even where the exegetical arguments take place in a translated form.[25]

The LXX influence on the composition of the New Testament and on the early church's access to the Jewish Scriptures is beyond dispute textually and historically. The simple point registered here,

---

disciple of Hillel (or perhaps Hillel himself) gave graphic expression to the principle behind this exegetical exercise: הפוך בה והפוך בה דכולה בה, "Turn it over again and again for everything is contained in it (i.e., in the Torah)."

25. Lim, *Formation*, 169; Brevard S. Childs, *Biblical Theology of the Old and New Testaments: Theological Reflection on the Christian Bible* (Minneapolis: Fortress, 1992), 62. Gallagher and Meade (*Biblical Canon Lists*, 21) quote James VanderKam, who claims that "both the Pharisees and Jesus assume the question they are discussing is to be answered from the scriptures." Given the shared canonical instincts with Pharisaic Judaism, the New Testament use of the LXX, or more simply, Greek translations, does not indicate a "broader" canon as this pertains to canonical scope, i.e., the Deuterocanonicals, or Apocrypha. Van der Toorn's insight above is worth repeating: the notion of a Greek Bible is a later construct (*Scribal Culture*, 262). The matter is more pedestrian: the Hebrew text is translatable and as translation can render its divine witness.

however, is a resistance to a potential non sequitur. The argument goes something like this: given the overwhelming evidence for the centrality of the LXX to early Christian thought, it follows, therefore, that the church's Old Testament was and is the LXX.[26] On the surface, such a statement may seem as obvious as the nose on our face. But perhaps the nose is an ear. Why? Because the formative role of the LXX in the early church speaks to the fact that God's Word is translatable, thus not supporting a privileged status of one particular translation in the economy of grace. Yes, God spoke Greek, as a good book on the LXX in the early church has recently reminded us.[27] But God also speaks Russian, German, Swahili, and, of course, English too.

Broad or Narrow Canon?

Questions pertaining to the LXX and the MT, the former witnessing to a broader Old Testament canon and the latter limiting its scope in concert with the Jewish synagogue, divide the Christian church to this day. As students of early church history know, this matter was of some consequence in a dispute between Augustine of Hippo and Jerome in the fifth century. Augustine argues for the inspiration of the original Hebrew Scriptures and the Septuagintal translators. As was the custom in his day, Augustine affirms the tradition communicated in the Letter of Aristeas that the seventy-two translators miraculously produced these translations in seventy

26. The church fathers' reliance on the Septuagint was due in part to their belief in the miraculous character of the translation and its fidelity to the original, beliefs whose origin can be traced to the Letter of Aristeas. See the history of this letter and its rabbinic and Christian reception in Wasserstein and Wasserstein, *Legend*. Michael Graves provides a helpful clarification, given the Septuagint's role in early Christian thought and practice: "Most Church Fathers did not intend to choose the Septuagint over the original Hebrew, but they assumed that the Septuagint captured the precise meaning of the original. Since most of these individuals did not know Hebrew, they were never confronted with the actual differences between the Hebrew text and the Septuagint." *Inspiration and Interpretation*, 103.

27. Law, *When God Spoke Greek*.

days.[28] Jerome, on the other hand, places the weight of canonical authority with the *Hebraica Veritas*, recognizing the LXX for
what it is: a translation.[29] Later, the magisterial Reformers and
their progeny sided with Jerome, while the Church of Rome (and
eventually the East) aligned with Augustine. To the present day,
the scope of the Christian canon remains a matter of ecclesiastical
and theological difference among various communions.

The differences between Jerome and Augustine on the priority
of the Hebrew or Greek textual traditions resist easy negotiation
because these matters are now a part of various ecclesiastical
identities. It is this historical phenomenon that led Childs to a
particular conclusion: "In sum, the exact nature of the Christian

28. In *City of God* 18.44, Augustine writes:
Without comparing both the Hebrew and Greek texts, however, we cannot
identify those passages which, while not being omitted or added, are differently
expressed: passages which either give another meaning, although one not at
odds with the original, or which can be shown to express the same meaning, but
in a different way. If, therefore, we see, as we should, nothing in those Scriptures
other than what the Spirit of God has spoken through men, it follows that
whatever is found in the Hebrew texts but not in the Septuagint is something
which the Spirit of God chose not to say through the translators, but only
through the prophets. Likewise, whatever is found in the Septuagint but not
in the Hebrew texts is something which the same Spirit chose to say through
the translators rather than through the prophets, thus showing that both the
former and the latter were prophets. . . . For just as the one Spirit of peace was
present in the prophets when they spoke the truth with no disagreement, so
also was the same one Spirit present in the seventy translators when, without
consulting one another, they still translated the whole as if with one voice.
(trans. R. W. Dyson, Cambridge Texts in the History of Political Thought
[Cambridge: Cambridge University Press, 1998])
See also Augustine's appeal to providence in *Christian Instruction* 2.15.
29. Augustine's understanding of language with its distinction between *signum
et res* (sign and reality) draws back from the predication of *veritas* on anything other
than the *res* of Scripture—namely, God himself. Jerome's linking of "truth" with the
Hebrew language is a theological problem for Augustine. In other words, Augustine's
reaction against Jerome is not solely indebted to his naive assumption about the miraculous character of the LXX. Jerome never denounced the LXX but continued to
make use of it, even when he believed his own translation of the Hebrew was more
successful. See Eva Schulz-Flügel, "The Latin Old Testament Tradition," in *Hebrew
Bible / Old Testament: The History of Its Interpretation*, vol. 1, *From the Begin-
nings to the Middle Ages (until 1300)*, ed. Magne Saebø (Göttingen: Vandenhoeck
& Ruprecht, 1996), 659–62.

Bible both in respect to its scope and text remain undecided to this day."[30] The division between Protestant and Catholic accounts of the canon's scope cannot be adjudicated by appeal to historical data alone. The points of division reside in the arena of theological instincts, particularly as this relates to the ordering of Word and Tradition. Recognizing the theological distinctions between Rome and Geneva at this critical juncture led Childs to one of the more provocative statements in his *Biblical Theology*: "Perhaps the basic theological issue at stake can be best formulated in terms of the church's ongoing *search* for the Christian Bible."[31] For Childs, this "search for the Christian Bible" will not be settled once and for all. Rather, it is the task of the church to give continual, critical, and theological reflection to its own ecclesiastical location and the normative character of Scripture as the rule of faith by which its life and doctrine is measured.[32]

The issue at hand turns full circle at this point. For Childs's search comes undone if canon and Scripture are formally distinguished.[33] As Ulrich argues, the notion of an "open canon" does not make sense under the constraints of "canon as list." If, however, Scripture functions canonically as the rule of faith for Christian life and doctrine despite questions at the margins regarding the canon's scope, then the settling of the canon's scope is not determinative of the canonical role that Scripture plays even when levels of uncertainty at the margins remain.[34] The historical data from the early church suggest that this distinction between canonical authority and canonical fixity was fully operational. Both the apostolic witness and early Christian theologians could

30. Childs, *Biblical Theology*, 63.
31. Childs, *Biblical Theology*, 67.
32. See Gignilliat, "God Speaks Hebrew."
33. See the discussion in chap. 1.
34. On canonical authority as distinguished from canonical fixity, see esp. Stephen Chapman, "Second Temple Jewish Hermeneutics: How Canon Is Not an Anachronism," in *Invention, Rewriting, Usurpation: Discursive Fights over Religious Traditions in Antiquity*, ed. J. Ulrich, A.-C. Jacobsen, and D. Brakke, Early Christianity in the Context of Antiquity 11 (Frankfurt: Peter Lang, 2012), 281–96.

HEBREW OR GREEK OR BOTH? The translations of the Hebrew Scriptures into Greek remain a significant historical and theological phenomenon. Undoubtedly the Septuagint (LXX) played a formative role in the shaping of the New Testament and early Christianity. The evidence suggests that this historical accident tells much about the translatability of the Old Testament, but it does not necessarily place the Septuagint translation above its Hebrew parent text.

appeal to Scripture canonically as the location and guarantor of truth without reservation. And this is true despite ongoing historical debates about which books in the Writings (*Ketuvim*) were understood as canonical in the first and second centuries AD.[35] If language of an open canon can be helpful at all, then it is most likely at this critical juncture: an affirmation that the Scriptures of Israel functioned authoritatively despite questions about the canon's scope or fixity at particular moments.[36]

Conclusion

For clarity's sake, a few matters should be kept before the reader. First, the appeal to Septuagint-like texts—or better, Greek translations in the New Testament or early church—does not require us to affirm a broader canonical scope. To put the matter in other terms, Paul can quote Septuagint Isaiah as an authoritative word while at the same time denying the scriptural (γραφή) character of, say, Judith. The evidence of Paul's appeal to Scripture in his letters suggests that such was indeed the case.

35. On the fundamental grammar of the Old Testament canon as "Law and Prophets," with the Writings finding their canonical role in light of the anterior character of the former, see esp. Christopher R. Seitz, *The Goodly Fellowship of the Prophets: The Achievement of Association in Canon Formation* (Grand Rapids: Baker Academic, 2009). For a maximal account of canonical fixity by the first century AD, see the essays in *The Shape of the Writings*, ed. J. Steinberg and T. Stone, Siphrut 16 (Winona Lake, IN: Eisenbrauns, 2015).

36. Seitz, *Goodly Fellowship*, 30.

Second and as just mentioned, whether in Greek or Hebrew form, the New Testament authors quote as Scripture the Old Testament books within the Hebrew canon to the exclusion of the extra books found in the Septuagint.[37] This is a matter of some consequence and is materially related to the first point made above: quotations that are LXX-like do not necessitate affirming a canonical scope that is broader than the Masoretic tradition. The quotation of Enoch in Jude 14–15 provides possible evidence for an exception that proves the rule.[38] At the same time, this observation about the scope of the New Testament's quotation of the Old Testament is part and parcel of the compositional history of the New Testament itself. In other words, New Testament practice may be suggestive but is not necessarily normative for church practice. As Childs reminds us in other contexts, "We are not apostles and prophets."

The third point is more theological in nature. Though divergent in hermeneutical approach, the church and the synagogue share a common canonical legacy pertaining to the Old Testament / Hebrew Scriptures. Texts such as Rom. 1:4–5 and 9:5 and the entire Old Testament witness to the unique role Israel plays in the divine economy. The covenant, the law, and the promises have been given and entrusted to the Jews. Therefore, the Jews' role as tradents of the canonical Scriptures remains of singular importance when wrestling with the theological priority of the Hebrew Bible or the Septuagint. Childs clarifies, "Therefore to use a different collection of Old Testament writings from those accepted by the Jews appeared as a threat to the theological continuity of the people of God. Had not Clement and Justin based their argument on the identity of the God of the Old Testament with the Father of

37. Sixteenth- and seventeenth-century Protestant scholastics made much of the same point in their debates with Rome about the Apocrypha. See Richard A. Muller, *Post-Reformation Reformed Dogmatics: The Rise and Development of Reformed Orthodoxy, ca. 1520 to ca. 1725*, vol. 2, *Holy Scripture: The Cognitive Foundation of Theology*, 2nd ed. (Grand Rapids: Baker Academic, 2003), 390.

38. See Gallagher and Meade, *Biblical Canon Lists*, 28–29.

Jesus Christ on the assumption of a common scripture between
church and synagogue?"[39] The authority of the Jewish Scriptures
in the life of the early church was not a matter of dispute. In fact,
as Hans von Campenhausen memorably frames the matter, the
early church struggled to come to terms with the identity of Jesus
given the anterior authority of the Hebrew Scriptures, even if in
translated form, and not vice versa.[40]

These questions about the scope of the canon are difficult matters with ecumenical consequences, the likes of which will not be
solved here. Those with Protestant instincts may find the arguments of the magisterial Reformers and their theological progeny
regarding the priority of the Hebrew canon persuasive, especially
as this relates to the sharing of the same canonical legacy between
synagogue and church. The material form of the canon as Old
and New Testaments reflects a theological continuity between the
Testaments.[41] Moreover, the Reformation instinct *ad fontes* (to the
sources) prioritizes the Hebrew Scriptures over the Septuagint,
a prioritization whose progenitors can be traced back through
the medieval period and beyond, even to Jerome.[42] Such a claim

39. Childs, *Biblical Theology*, 65. Seventeenth-century Reformed orthodox theo-
logian Francis Turretin makes much of this argument in his own affirmation of the
Hebrew canon's priority vis-à-vis other translations of it. In fact, his first argument
against the inclusion of the apocryphal books is "(1) The Jewish church, to which
the oracles of God were committed (Rom. 3:2), never considered them as canonical,
but held the same canon with us." Turretin continues, "Nor should the canon of the
Jews be distinguished here from that of Christians because Christians neither can nor
ought to receive other books of the Old Testament as canonical than those which they
received from the Jews, their book-servants 'who carry the books of us students.'"
Turretin's final quote is from Augustine on Ps. 40. *Institutes of Elenctic Theology*,
ed. J. T. Dennison Jr., trans. G. M. Giger (Phillipsburg, NJ: P&R, 1992), 1:102–3.

40. Hans von Campenhausen, *The Formation of the Christian Bible*, trans. J. A.
Baker (Mifflintown, PA: Sigler, 1997), 21. See also Robert W. Jenson, *Canon and
Creed*, Interpretation: Resources for the Use of Scripture in the Church (Louisville:
Westminster John Knox, 2010), 22.

41. Childs, *Biblical Theology*, 74.

42. The rise of Hebrew knowledge in the medieval period became a critical tool for
textual critics of the time. Frans van Liere describes one such medieval textual critic,
Andrew of St. Victor (d. 1175), as follows: "As a way of detecting and correcting errors
in the text, he frequently referred to the Hebrew text of the Old Testament, which

maintains its theological force despite the undeniable influence of the Septuagint on early Christian thought. Recognizing the early LXX influences speaks to the operative work of the Holy Spirit via the scriptural word in translated form, a matter whose theological implications invite continued reflection regarding the relationship of the operative work of the Spirit with the biblical text and the fixity of language itself.[43] On the other hand, those whose theological sympathies are on the far side of the Rubicon may align themselves with Augustine's arguments about the coequal status of tradition and Scripture, reifying the early church's broad use of the Septuagint as normative for later Christian practice. Perhaps Childs's summation regarding the continual "search for the Christian Bible" best describes the ecclesial situation in the West as Protestants and Catholics continue in conversation with one another regarding the church's canonical legacy.

---

he presumably knew through the oral contacts with Jews in Paris. His commentaries were a trove of valuable information to later scholars who set out to produce a Latin Bible text that was more in line with the Hebrew 'original.'" *An Introduction to the Medieval Bible* (Cambridge: Cambridge University Press, 2014), 99.

43. Robert Jenson frames the matter well with his typical laconic style: "My theory can be quickly stated: strictly speaking, the canonical text of the Old Testament is neither the Hebrew nor the Greek by itself, but both texts together and either text if need be. Practice will then depend on the situation with a particular passage. When we can discover reasonable grounds for supposing that one or the other text is 'better,' by any of the rules usual among textual critics, that is the canonical text. When this is not possible, we should refuse to choose and interpret both." Jenson's instincts are Augustinian regarding the coauthoritative status of Hebrew and Greek texts. On the other hand, his affirmation of textual criticism allows for the possibility that one text is to be preferred above another. Even here, however, Jenson's text-critical logic may not be clear. For the Septuagint's important role in textual criticism is as a witness to a different Hebrew *Vorlage*, if the goal of textual criticism is as Tov has suggested: the establishment of the final form of a biblical book (Jenson, *Canon and Creed*, 62). Jenson's final comments on the subject, despite the lack of clarity regarding the Septuagint's role in textual criticism, are of value, especially as this pertains to the role of translations in the divine economy. "But how can the fixity definitive of a Scripture be independent of a fixity of language? It is possible only if we again trust the Spirit. We must trust the purposes of the Spirit both in history that leads to the dual text, and in the problem with which he thus leaves us" (62).

Part 2

SCRIPTURE'S
SUBJECT MATTER

5

God as Triune, and Exegetical Metaphysics

Historicism: The term refers to an intellectual movement whose focus is the particularities of peoples, places, and cultures in their historical moment in time. It leans against the tendency to speak of ideas and ethics in universal terms, preferring concrete forms of human thinking, feeling, and acting in their place and time.

Metaphysics: In this chapter, the appeal to metaphysics is modest. It does not necessitate a particular metaphysical theory, such as participationist or voluntarist. Rather, metaphysics entails a theological commitment to the being of God as necessary for sense-making in our world. In brief, metaphysics refers to the ordering of reality by an understanding of God as creator and redeemer.

Trinitarian logic: God reveals himself in Scripture as singular in substance; there is one God. God reveals himself in Scripture as a plurality of persons, differentiated in relation but not in substance. The Father is not the Son, and so forth. The substance/relation distinction is necessary for coming to terms with Scripture's presentation of God's being and identity.

By now readers have a good sense that the approach offered in this book necessitates confessional commitments: the providence of

God in the literary affairs of creatures, canon understood first and foremost as an internal property of the biblical texts, Scripture as the fitting means by which God reveals himself to humanity, and the list continues. These theological commitments aid readers of Scripture in their understanding of the material character of the Christian Bible. They not only aid but also make possible an understanding of Scripture's "whatness" (quiddity). What one might consider basic interpretive questions put to any text—such as "Who wrote this?" and "What are the causes leading to these textual effects?"—are not detached from theological commitments when attending to the Old Testament as Christian Scripture.

As Thomas Aquinas affirmed so long ago, Scripture's literal sense is rendered by the intention of its author.[1] With modern ears, such a statement seems par for the course for those who still affirm some account of texts as differentiated from readers. Yet, Aquinas continues, Scripture's author is God. From a Christian theological view, no other text can make such a claim about its author. So who then is the God of the Old Testament, and what are the interpretive implications of naming him as Scripture's primary author? This chapter and the next turn toward these more formal matters as they seek to identify Scripture's primary author and the interpretative implications stemming from this authorial identification.

Conversational Challenges

Before turning to the theoretical and practical, I will illustrate the problem that Bible scholars and theologians have with each other when entering this conversation. I do so because I believe there are suspicions lurking on each side. Some time ago I presented a paper at a university on the theological character of a theological commentary. In retrospect, it was not a very good paper, but I was working my way through some account of a theological

1. Thomas Aquinas, *Summa Theologiae* 1.1.10.

commentary that set itself over against the dominant historicist approach of biblical scholars (more of this in a bit). Afterward a Bible scholar whom I respect said to me, "I read my text closely in its historical context by means of close philological and contextual study. I take seriously what the text says about God as indicative of who God is and do not reduce God-talk of the Scripture to a religiohistorical phenomenon locked in an ancient anthropology. Then I talk about God on the basis of this text. Please tell me, what is not theological about my reading?" I am paraphrasing this gentlemen's inquiry, but this retelling, I think, gets at the heart of his concerns.

The second illustration draws from a spate of book reviews by Walter Moberly regarding theological hermeneutics. For example, in his review of Scott Swain's monograph on trinitarian herme-neutics, Moberly, almost predictably, laments the varied instincts that theologians and Bible scholars bring to the critical relation of theology and exegesis.[2] Bible scholars, Moberly claims, cannot avoid the details of the text by means of theological elaboration or never-ending discussions about hermeneutics. Biblical scholars need to wrestle with genocide and knotty textual details, while theologians can wander the mountain ranges of theory and herme-neutics. Moberly has a legitimate concern about the dangers of ever speaking of theological exegesis without attendant engage-ment with the details of biblical texts. Though I believe Moberly overstates his case with Swain, his overarching concerns remain valid: texts need to be handled.

Why these two stories? Because they illustrate the concerns this chapter seeks to address regarding the relation of speculative theology and close readings of the biblical text. They illustrate the challenges that confessional exegesis confronts when it seeks to order its thoughts in accord with God's revealed identity as

2. Walter Moberly, "Review of Scott R. Swain, *Trinity, Revelation, and Reading: A Theological Introduction to the Bible and Its Interpretation*," *International Journal of Systematic Theology* 17 (2015): 351–54.

triune while at the same time attending to the details of the text's literary and semantic features. First, I want to think about the nature of confession, and how confession shapes our metaphysical understanding of language. How has historicism problematized the relation between metaphysical commitments and biblical language? Also, why is talk about "God" not sufficient for a Christian engagement with Holy Scripture if such talk is not tethered to trinitarian discourse? Second, and drawing from Moberly's concerns, texts need to be handled in the particularity of their verbal and poetic character. Freewheeling hermeneutical reflections apart from the nitty-gritty details of textual engagement run counter to the material sufficiency of Scripture. Texts and their language matter. At the same time, biblical texts cannot be separated from their subject matter. The rise of historicism in the Western intellectual tradition poses serious threats to the necessary relation between the biblical text and its divine subject matter.

Historicism and the Challenge of Language and Referent

The German historicist tradition entered the philosophical stage with force after the demise of Hegel's long reign in the German philosophical tradition. Frederick Beiser provides a compelling narrative of philosophy's fight for existence in university life during the last half of the nineteenth century because of the dominant interest in the natural sciences.[3] The natural sciences gave pause to the intelligentsia of the day regarding the necessity of philosophy as a stand-alone discipline. The questions of philosophy appeared to be answered by the results of the natural sciences, resulting in some disciplinary gaps that needed to be filled. Enter the materialist controversies. Enter Schopenhauer. And more germane to our subject matter, enter the historicist tradition.[4]

3. Frederick C. Beiser, *After Hegel: German Philosophy, 1840–1890* (Princeton: Princeton University Press, 2014).
4. Beiser, *After Hegel*, chap. 1.

Historicism, as an intellectual movement, arose in response to the search for transcendent warrant for moral, political, and societal values. In other words, although the Enlightenment had rejected the classic Christian metaphysic where God and God's providential ordering of history toward his own ends played center court, it had not rejected metaphysics outright. Rather, it sought to ground metaphysics in universal principles of reason located in the rational and ordered inquiry of humanity. These universal principles are irrespective of historically particular places, times, or cultures. *Historicism rejects outright both Christian and Enlightenment metaphysics, resisting any account of the transcendent apart from the particularities of place, time, and culture.*

In his insightful book *The German Historicist Tradition*, Beiser points out that historicism as a philosophical movement operated with the playbook of its nominalist forebears.[5] Nominalism arose as a countermovement to the dominance of Aristotelian modes of thinking in the late medieval period. Like nineteenth-century historicism, late-medieval nominalism also rejected universals in favor of particulars. Or put in other terms, universals were concepts of the mind (thus "conceptualist") based on perceptions of shared relations. However, according to Richard Cross, substance is numerically one and singular in Ockhamist nominalism.[6] Existence resides in the particular and concrete, not in the abstract or ideal, as in Aristotelian thought. In other words, *forms are material things.* As Beiser summarizes,

5. Frederick C. Beiser, *The German Historicist Tradition* (Oxford: Oxford University Press, 2011), 5.

6. Richard Cross, *The Medieval Christian Philosophers: An Introduction* (New York: Tauris, 2014), 190. Radner makes a compelling case for the potential of figural reading from either participationist metaphysics or a metaphysics of omnipotence (Ockham). Ephraim Radner, *Time and the Word: Figural Reading of the Christian Scriptures* (Grand Rapids: Eerdmans, 2016), 160–61. It should be noted, according to Radner's account et al., that Ockham's understanding of the singularity of substance does not necessitate a strict literalist reading of Scripture. Ockham's metaphysics of omnipotence allowed for such (152).

The meaning and purpose of a thought, intention, value or belief did not exist apart from the determinate context, actions and words that expressed or embodied it. Since these expressions and embodiments are so different, indeed incommensurable, there cannot be a single form of human nature, reason or value. To talk about reason, value or human nature in general, apart from their specific expressions or embodiments in a specific time and place, is to indulge in mere abstractions.[7]

Historicism as a philosophical movement shares much in common with its nominalist great-grandfather. As a philosophical movement, it rejects metaphysics of both the theistic/Christian type and the Enlightenment kind. As Beiser concludes, "The fundamental principle of historicism is that all human actions and ideas have to be explained historically according to their specific historical causes and contexts."[8]

Beiser's book is some five-hundred-plus pages of densely researched argument regarding the character, scope, and principal figures of the German historicist tradition, ranging from Johann Martin Chladenius and Johann Gottfried Herder through Wilhelm Humboldt and Wilhelm Dilthey to Max Weber. This brief account (above) barely scratches the surface of historicism's philosophical legacy. Nevertheless, I think we have enough of the

7. Beiser, *Historicist Tradition*, 5.

8. Beiser, *Historicist Tradition*, 19. There are approaches to this matter other than the metaphysical (though I think from a Christian theological perspective this is the preferred tack). In *Truth and Method* (New York: Bloomsbury Academic, 2013), Hans-Georg Gadamer speaks of the implicit problems of historicism and romantic psychological approaches in their sealing off texts from their reception and effects (*Wirkung*). Temporal distance, in Gadamer's terms, is not something that must be overcome (308). Gadamer links this notion with the "naïve assumption of historicism." Rather, temporal distance creates the necessary conditions because the "yawning abyss" is filled with the continuity of custom and tradition. In an important point, Gadamer claims: "The positive conditions of historical understanding include the relative closure of a historical event, which allows us to view it as a whole, and its distance from contemporary opinions concerning its import" (309). Gadamer's "fusion of horizons" is born out of these reflections. There seems to be compatibility between this view and the privileging of the text's final form on offer in this book.

picture before us to begin to see the massive impact that historicist modes of thinking have had on biblical studies in the academy and the church. Modern biblical criticism is a rich and varied thing, whose results provide important avenues of inquiry and appreciation for Scripture's linguistic, poetic, and historical depth. But somewhere lurking in the shadows, or perhaps dancing in full view, is the historicist resistance to metaphysics as a critical tool for reading historical texts. Brian Daley does not dance around the issue when he claims that historical criticism often operates as "*methodologically* atheistic."[9] John Webster expresses it this way: "Once the *historia scripturae* is allowed to be determinative of the way in which the ontology of Scripture is conceived, then the biblical texts become a sub-set of the larger category of 'texts in general.'"[10] The seemingly safer ground of evangelical historical-grammatical readings does not escape these historicist concerns either.

Christian Metaphysics and Biblical Language

If scriptural texts such as the Old Testament are reduced to their particular historical moment or textual history, hemmed in by the epistemic constraints of author, editor, and initial audience(s), we run the risk of collapsing metaphysics/ontology and epistemology into each other: what the human author knew constrains the metaphysical reach of what the human author wrote. The collapsing of these two related but distinct categories runs into a very real danger. It muddles how we understand biblical language and its referential character. As Webster frames the matter, "In Christian theological usage, Scripture is

9. Brian E. Daley, "Is Patristic Exegesis Still Usable? Some Reflections on Early Christian Interpretation of the Psalms," in *The Art of Reading Scripture*, ed. E. F. Davis and R. B. Hays (Grand Rapids: Eerdmans, 2003), 72.

10. John Webster, "Resurrection and Scripture," in *Christology and Scripture: Interdisciplinary Perspectives*, ed. A. T. Lincoln and A. Paddison (London: T&T Clark, 2008), 145.

an ontological category; to speak of the Bible as Holy Scripture is to indicate what it *is*."[11] Webster presses the matter further: "To say 'Scripture' is to say 'revelation'—not just in the sense that these texts are to be handled *as if* they were bearers of divine revelation, but in the sense that revelation is fundamental to the texts' *being*."[12] If such a formal claim is made about Scripture's ontology or its "whatness," it naturally follows to speak of the ontological or metaphysical dimension attendant to the material character of Scripture: the Bible is composed of language/words within the scope of a two-Testament canon.[13] So what then about language? My reflections here will be brief and my interlocutors selective; astute readers will be aware of the plenitude of resources and scholarly discussion on the philosophy of language and hermeneutics.[14]

In his Gifford Lectures, *The Edge of Words*, Rowan Williams reminds us of the enormous reach of human language. "We are always saying more than we entirely grasp."[15] He describes this phenomenon of human language with a pregnant phrase: "the

11. Webster, "Resurrection," 144.

12. Webster, "Resurrection," 144.

13. The reciprocal relationship between literary semantics and Scripture's trinitarian subject matter is especially evident in Luther's Old Testament exegesis. In her insightful examination of Luther's trinitarian hermeneutic, Christine Helmer shows how Luther tethers himself to the Hebrew text and language itself as the "vehicle for trinitarian knowledge." "Luther's Trinitarian Hermeneutic and the Old Testament," *Modern Theology* 18 (2002): 55. The Holy Spirit as teaching and authorial agent of Israel's Scriptures opens up the tangible and fixed character of the Hebrew text to the divine mystery. In Helmer's terms, "Hebrew is the language the Spirit uses to refer to a theological subject matter" (55). Of significance here is Luther's close attention to the Hebrew text and the peculiarities of its syntactical/lexical idiom as "a first step in grasping the trinitarian reality" (55). Helmer concludes, "With respect to the Trinity, the only material is the letter that points beyond itself, to a subject matter in eternity" (65).

14. See, e.g., Charles Taylor, *The Language Animal: The Full Shape of the Human Linguistic Capacity* (Cambridge, MA: Belknap Press of Harvard University Press, 2016).

15. Rowan Williams, *The Edge of Words: God and the Habits of Language* (London: Bloomsbury, 2014), 167. Williams describes the silence of our speech—when we stop thinking, speaking, or imagining—as stemming not from a void but from plenitude.

hinterland of significance."[16] Williams's lectures are a stunning and beautiful account of the ability of human language to describe and represent, while remaining fully aware that these activities of language are never sealed off from the potential for re-presentation or description via new modes and tropes of discourse. Williams speaks of the "unfinished character of language."[17] We re-present with our words, and the task of re-presentation is never once for all. French phenomenologist Merleau-Ponty makes a similar claim about painting: "For painters, if any remain, the world will always be yet to be painted; even if it lasts millions of years, . . . it will all end without having been complete."[18] For painting as well as for language, there is always more; the object is never finally grasped.

When Williams speaks of the "hinterland of significance," he is referring to our normal modes of discourse through the language games we play while communicating and sense-making in our world. If we speak this way about human language and discourse in "ordinary language," how much more so do we understand the potential of biblical language, even with its apparent fixity, to "say more."[19] As mentioned already in the introduction to this chapter, Aquinas appeals to the authority of Scripture's authorial intentionality, quickly clarifying who the author of Scripture is: God.

George Steiner joins the chorus of those who understand the expansive borders of human language to "say more." "A sentence always means more."[20] Steiner clarifies, "The informing matrix or context of even a rudimentary, literal proposition—and just what does *literal* mean?—moves outward from specific utterance or notation in ever-widening concentric and overlapping circles. These

---

16. Williams, *Edge of Words*, 167.

17. Williams, *Edge of Words*, 168.

18. Maurice Merleau-Ponty, "Eye and Mind," in *The Merleau-Ponty Aesthetics Reader: Philosophy and Painting*, ed. G. A. Johnson, trans. M. B. Smith (Evanston, IL: Northwestern University Press, 1993), 148.

19. On "ordinary language," see the essays in Stanley Cavell, *Must We Mean What We Say?* (Cambridge: Cambridge University Press, 2002).

20. George Steiner, *Real Presences* (Chicago: University of Chicago Press, 1989), 82.

comprise the individual, subconsciously quickened language habits and *associative field-mappings* of the particular speaker or
writer."[21] This expansive character of language reveals, in Steiner's
terms, "the incommensurability of the semantic."[22] Put in more
available terms, literature is loaded with semantic potential.

Much more could and should be said here about language and
the metaphysics of being. But one point from Steiner is worth capi-
talizing on for the sake of this book's focus on the Old Testament
and its trinitarian subject matter. For Steiner, a sentence always
means more because of the generative potential of "associative-
field mapping": a concept worth conscripting into the service of
our discussion. The verbal character of the Old Testament, a verbal
character worthy of respect in the idiom of the Old Testament's
material form, is in associative relationship with the whole of the
Christian Bible, Old and New Testaments. Its sentences mean
more—if by "meaning more" we mean go beyond the epistemic
horizons of the authors and editors—because of the associative-
field mapping of a two-Testament witness centered on a single
subject matter and single authorial voice. Put in pedestrian terms,
God was not waiting till Matt. 1:1 to make himself triune.

The triune identity of God emerging from Scripture's total
witness pressures Christian readers to yield to the hermeneutical
significance of Paul's claim in Colossians: "And he [Jesus Christ] is
before all things" (Col. 1:17). "Before all things" certainly includes
the Old Testament canon. Such a claim about God's being as triune, self-communicative, and self-revealing resists the reduction
of Holy Scripture's semantic reach to the epistemic horizons of
those involved in the compositional and textual history of the Old
Testament canon—whether with abstract categories or descrip-
tors, like "God" apart from triune identification of that God, or in
seemingly faithful approaches like "Christotelism" (Christ as the
telos/goal of the Old Testament promises). Christotelic readings

21. Steiner, *Real Presences*, 82.
22. Steiner, *Real Presences*, 83.

run into the danger of fusing the ontological character of Israel's Scripture with the epistemic horizon of those who wrote, edited, and compiled them. Even though Moses might not have been a self-conscious trinitarian, we can be assured that God was.

When Isaiah or Moses or Jeremiah utter a prophetic word, do not their language and verbal expressions say more than they could grasp? Are the patterns of their poetic and linguistic choices in the givenness of their literary form also linked with the "incommensurability of the semantic"? Does the whole Christian canon as a two-Testament witness pressure us to see the Old Testament's subject as our Triune God, with the Tetragrammaton (the divine name YHWH) as best predicated on the essence of God revealed in the tripersonal naming of God as Father, Son, and Holy Spirit (more of this in the next chapter)? Does such a claim allow the Old Testament to remain a Christian witness even beyond the ways the New Testament hears it because "[Christ] is before all things"? Or are we working, again, with an overly historicist account of the Old Testament that reduces its theological witness to the epistemic constraints of its moment in the divine economy?

When Jean-Luc Marion claimed, "The body of the text does not belong to the text, but to the One who is embodied in it," he was speaking of theological writing that moves from Word to words.[23] The Word finds a body in the text. If such is the case, how much more so does his claim ring true in our hermeneutical approaches to Scripture that move from Word to words for the sake of rereading—or perhaps better, reencountering—the Word embodied in the language of the Old Testament witness?

While commenting on John 1:18, Aquinas speaks of the trinitarian implications of the Word coming to the prophets: "For in the past, the only begotten Son revealed knowledge of God through the prophets, who made him known to the extent that they shared in the eternal Word. Hence they said things like, *the*

---

23. Jean-Luc Marion, *God without Being*, trans. T. A. Carlson, 2nd ed. (Chicago: University of Chicago Press, 2012), 1.

Word of the Lord came to me."[24] The personal agency of the Word as that which comes to the prophets in created form, as word(s), adumbrates the unique moment in the divine economy when the Word "became flesh" (John 1:14). The giving of the Word in the creaturely medium of human language anticipates and witnesses to the singularity of that moment when in the fullness of time God takes on flesh: the incarnation (Heb. 1:1).

Therefore, the prophetic word of the Old Testament is an extension of Yhwh's own revealed self, fitted as it is to the singularity of the divine being in tripersonal relation. Put in the terms set out in this chapter, such a trinitarian account of biblical language necessitates that Old Testament texts can "say more." The source of the Bible's language is the infinite plenitude of the divine being, revealing himself by means of the Word's agency. Moreover, Old Testament language can "say more" within the confines of the texts' own literary stability and final form as they witness to the Scripture's semantic plenitude. A brief look at the prophetic description of Isaiah's servant in Isa. 52:13 will serve to illustrate the theoretical account of language presented in this section.

The Servant: High and Exalted (*rum wenisa*', Isa. 52:13)

An unfolding occurs in the description of Isaiah's servant in Isa. 40–55. Put simply, this unfolding centers on the following question: "Who is the servant?" Or, "Is Israel the servant?" The presentation of the material in Isa. 40–48 leaves little doubt regarding the answer to these questions. The servant is Israel, period. Isaiah 41:8 suffices: "But you, Israel, my servant, Jacob, whom I have chosen, the offspring of Abraham, my friend." The servant *is* Israel; Israel *is* the servant.

---

24. Thomas Aquinas, *Commentary on the Gospel of John: Chapters 1–8*, Biblical Commentaries 35 (Lander, WY: Aquinas Institute for the Study of Sacred Doctrine), chap. 1, lect. 11, §221, https://dhspriory.org/thomas/John1.htm.

A shift occurs in the servant's description after the critical juncture of Isa. 48. In this chapter it is declared that "from this time forth I announce to you new things, hidden things that you have not known. They are created now, not long ago" (48:6–8). After this announcement of "new things," the prophetic word moves to the second of the so-called Servant Songs, in Isa. 49. Indeed, "new things" are occurring in chapter 49. Isaiah 49:3 clearly identifies the servant as Israel—no news here—and then Isa. 49:6 identifies servant Israel as having a mission *to* Israel: "to bring Jacob back to him, and that Israel might be gathered to him" (my trans.). The presentation of the servant's identity in Isa. 49 seems congruent with the following logic: The servant is Israel and at the same time distinct from Israel insofar as the servant has a mission *to* Israel. In other words, the identity and vocation of Israel becomes a garment ready to be worn by one able to take on this identity for the nations *and* for Israel. New things are unfolding in the economy of God's redemptive relating to his people.

When readers of Isa. 40–55 arrive at the last of the Servant Songs, Isa. 52:13–53:12, they are in for another surprise. This servant figure on the far side of the seismic shift of Isa. 48 is now described with language that catches the astute reader off guard. "Behold, my servant shall act wisely; he shall be *high* [יָרוּם] and . . . shall be exalted [וְנִשָּׂא]" (52:13). This collocation of terms is found in three other places in Isaiah.[25]

In the year that King Uzziah died, I saw the Lord, high [רָם] and exalted [וְנִשָּׂא]. (6:1 NIV)

"Now I will arise," says the LORD, "now I will lift myself up [יָרוּם]; now I will be exalted [imperfect 1st common sg. of נשׂא]." (33:10)

25. For the lexeme רום in Isaiah, cf. 1:2 (raised children); 2:12–13 (arrogance); 6:1; 10:33 (arrogance); 14:13 (Day Star of Babylon raising his throne); 25:1 (exalting the LORD God); 30:18 (God exalts himself to show mercy); 33:10 (I will raise and exalt); 52:13; 57:15.

For thus says the One who is high [רם] and lifted up [ונשא], who inhabits eternity, whose name is Holy: "I dwell in the high and holy place." (57:15)

These texts are all related to one another by intertextual association. And they all identify Yhwh as *rum* and *nasa'* by use of participial (attributive and substantive) and imperfective forms. In fact, throughout Isaiah the prophet deploys *rum* as a negative descriptor of Israel in the people's self-actualization and pride (Isa. 2:12–13; 10:33). Whenever Israel "exalts" itself, Yhwh as the great tree-feller turns to Israel, lopping off its prideful branches. Isaiah makes one thing clear: only Yhwh is *rum wenisa'*.

Careful readers are taken aback, then, when the servant is described as *rum wenisa'* in Isa. 52:13. At the beginning of the fourth Servant Song (Isa. 52:13–15), the servant is presented on the far side of his suffering as participating in the selfsame exaltation of Yhwh. The announcement is an act of prophetic prolepsis, alerting readers to the outcome of the suffering depicted in the following verses. The servant's description in 52:13 is distinct from Yhwh, the sending agent—"Behold, *my* servant"—and at the same time is sharing in the selfsame identity of Yhwh, the only One in Isaiah's prophetic corpus who is ever *rum wenisa'*. The verbal character of the text before us presses us to think in terms of trinitarian logic: singularity of divine essence in a plurality of personhood. Only Yhwh is *rum wenisa'*, yet the servant shares in this divine property while distinct in personhood from the sending agent.

Circling back to the previous discussion about language and metaphysics or language and theological ontology, I am not making a claim that Isaiah or "Deutero-Isaiah" or the tradent of the material intended a trinitarian claim in Isa. 52:13. I should say, I'm not necessarily denying that claim either, but the hermeneutical argument does not rest on their epistemic understanding.[26] I am

26. See Gadamer: "What is fixed in writing has detached itself from the contingency of its origin and its author and made itself free for new relationships. Normative concepts such as the author's meaning or the original reader's understanding in

making a different kind of claim. The language of the canonical text Isaiah, given the ontology of Scripture and given Isaiah's canonical location in a two-Testament canon, pressures us to think in trinitarian terms about this particular text in light of the text's literal sense and the Scripture's theological subject matter. In the broad stream of the Christian interpretive tradition, the appeal to the literal sense of Scripture necessitates the coequal affirmation of Scripture's theological subject matter: the literal sense and Scripture's subject matter resist dissolution. Can Isa. 52:13 be understood in ways that differ from this account? Certainly. But must it be and, moreover, should it be given the theoretical claims made above? Perhaps not.

Conclusion

During the 2016 fall semester, Samford University hosted an evening discussion on theology and the arts with Dan Siedell. After Siedell's presentation, a panel joined him to discuss the topic at hand. I was out of my element but captivated by the subject matter and discussion. While preparing for the evening, I was drawn to the work of the Postimpressionist artist Paul Cézanne. I have long had an amateurish interest in Impressionist and Postimpressionist paintings. But my grammar and vocabulary for expressing my appreciation could not press beyond surface comments like "Those sunflowers are really something."

The French phenomenologist Merleau-Ponty, however, helped give me a grammar for my appreciation of Cézanne in his essay "Cézanne's Doubt."[27] The essay also aids our understanding of the metaphysics of language, a metaphysics inherently related to the metaphysics of art. Merleau-Ponty recognizes that Cézanne was

---

fact represent only an empty space that is filled from time to time in understanding" (*Truth and Method*, 413).

27. Maurice Merleau-Ponty, "Cézanne's Doubt," in *The Merleau-Ponty Aesthetics Reader: Philosophy and Painting*, ed. G. A. Johnson, trans. M. B. Smith (Evanston, IL: Northwestern University Press, 1993), 59–75.

a troubled man. His unique ability to see the world and capture both the nature of the object itself along with the subjective perception of that object in an act of seeing marks the brilliance of Cézanne's artistic legacy. But as one might imagine, some critics reduce Cézanne to his mental neurosis.

Merleau-Ponty makes the following insightful claim: "Thus the 'hereditary traits,' the 'influence'—the accidents in Cézanne's life—are the text which nature and history gave him to decipher. They give only the literal meaning of his work. But an artist's creations, like a person's free decisions, impose on this given a figurative sense which did not exist before them."[28] In other words, we get to know Cézanne's work first and then through it understand the "literal sense" of his life more fully. "From the very start, Cézanne's life found its only equilibrium by leaning on his work that was still in the future. His life was the preliminary project of his future work."[29]

An analogue from Merleau-Ponty's description of Cézanne to the concerns of this chapter seems fitting. The verbal character of the Old Testament in its literal sense *opens up* to the future: much like the *literal sense* of Cézanne's life opens up to the future of his work. Yet in this *opening up*, the Old Testament's "life" or *literal sense* or given verbal form is not left behind for greener New Testament pastures. As Cézanne's paintings provide a necessary entry point to the fixity of his life, so too does the trinitarian subject matter of Scripture provide an entry point to the fixity of the Old Testament's verbal character. The mutually enforcing and enriching character of the language of Scripture and its trinitarian subject matter allows for a fuller appreciation of the Old Testament's range of signification.

28. Merleau-Ponty, "Cézanne's Doubt," 70.
29. Merleau-Ponty, "Cézanne's Doubt," 70.

6

The Trinity and the
Old Testament

Persona: This is a technical term in trinitarian discourse for the tri-personal mode of being within the Godhead. A distinction within the Trinity is made according to divine persons but not divine essence. These relational distinctions are also referred to as divine processions.

Ousia: "Of one *substance* with the Father" is the way Nicene orthodoxy defines the Son's divinity in relation to the Father's divinity. "Substance" is the translation of *ousia*. There is only one God whose substance or essence is singular: "*one* substance with the Father." A distinction exists between the persons of the Trinity in relation but not in substance or essence. Put simply, essence or substance refers to all that makes God God, allowing us to identify him as such.

The identification of Yhwh as the God whom Christians name Father, Son, and Holy Spirit remains a challenging subject for several reasons. A primary one observed in the previous chapter is historicism's hermeneutical legacy. The Old Testament's literal sense collapses onto its historical sense within this interpretive frame.[1]

---

1. See Brevard S. Childs, "The *Sensus Literalis* of Scripture: An Ancient and Modern Problem," in *Festschrift für Walther Zimmerli zum 70. Geburtstag* (Göttingen: Vandenhoeck & Ruprecht, 1977), 80–93.

Evangelical scholars tend to limit the historical sense to the named author(s) of Scripture, where such applies or can be responsibly reconstructed. Critical scholarship expands the historical sense to include various levels of tradition-critical and redaction-critical analysis. Despite the differences, evangelical and critical hermeneutical approaches share the interpretive instincts inherited from the rise of historical consciousness in the early eighteenth century.[2]

The previous claim is not intended as a pejorative comment per se. The benefits of modern criticism for the lexical and historical contextualization of Scripture aid modern readers in multiple ways. Scripture's so-called depth dimension, a textual phenomenon valorized in the modern period, is not necessarily at odds with a confessional understanding of Scripture, because it reflects the dynamically present character of the divine word to subsequent generations of readers/hearers.

This textual dynamic is present within the Scripture's own self-witness. Jeremiah, for example, appeals to Micah's prophecy for the sake of bolstering his own claims (Jer. 26:18). The *middot* (attributes) of God heralded in Exod. 34:6–7 weave their way through the Minor Prophets at critical interpretive junctures.[3] While compositional history and textual reception are related but distinct matters, the fact still remains that Scripture listens to Scripture in its own compositional history. These insights into Scripture's own internal cross association—"intertextuality" is the term du jour—help modern readers in multiple ways, the least of which is an appreciation for how Scripture's tradition-building process reveals a canon consciousness in the texts themselves. As observed

2. See Thomas Albert Howard, *Religion and the Rise of Historicism: W. M. L. De Wette, Jacob Burckhardt, and the Theological Origins of Nineteenth-Century Historical Consciousness* (Cambridge: Cambridge University Press, 2000). See also Frederick C. Beiser, *The German Historicist Tradition* (Oxford: Oxford University Press, 2011); Beiser, *After Hegel: German Philosophy, 1840–1890* (Princeton: Princeton University Press, 2014).

3. See Raymond C. Van Leeuwen, "Scribal Wisdom and Theodicy in the Book of the Twelve," in *In Search of Wisdom: Essays in Memory of John G. Gammie*, ed. L. G. Perdue, B. B. Scott, and W. J. Wiseman (Louisville: Westminster John Knox, 1993), 31–49.

in the first part of this book, canon is not an extrinsic imposition of later doctrinal formulas onto Scripture's self-witness but emerges from the text's own internal pressure.

All the historical advances of modernity notwithstanding, trinitarian readings of the Old Testament run into hermeneutical brick walls. I sought to surmount some of these walls in the previous chapter. How can texts written before the incarnation refer to metaphysical realities beyond the conceptual horizons of the human authors and tradents of the Old Testament? Was Moses a trinitarian? These kinds of questions are not new, raising their heads at various moments in the church's struggle to name its God. The hermeneutical question then remains straightforward. Is the Old Testament's trinitarian character grounded in the exegesis of Scripture itself, or does it amount to a homiletical or hermeneutical palimpsest imposed onto—rather than drawn from—Scripture's own self-witness? Moreover, if as Christians we affirm the triune character of our God, then a question regarding the identity of Yhwh in the Old Testament follows. Is Yhwh a *persona* of the divine essence or the *ousia* itself? Put in other terms, is Yhwh the Father or the divine essence of three *personae*?

Admittedly, these questions are enormous and of some consequence. The present chapter does not portend an exhaustive answer but will make initial and modest steps toward clarifying what it means to understand Yhwh as triune. Then I will explore the implications of this triune identification for our reading of the Old Testament. Our attention turns first to the identification of Israel's God as Yhwh.

Who Is Yhwh? Exodus and the Divine Name

The question "Who is God?" registers somewhere near the heart of the Old Testament's theological subject matter.[4] When Moses

---

4. The hesitation to identify *the* center of the Old Testament's theological witness is warranted.

encounters God at the burning bush, the matter of identifying his name comes to the fore (Exod. 3:13–14). "When they ask for your name, how shall I answer them?" (my trans.). God's reply to Moses's straightforward question remains a disputed matter to this day: אהיה אשר אהיה. "Tell them אהיה ["I am" or "I will be"] has sent you" (my trans.).

Coming to terms with the significance of this encounter and the connotative force of the name is no mean task. Along with the Septuagint and the majority of the Christian interpretive tradition—for good measure I will add Maimonides's name to the list—the revelation of God's name in Exod. 3 speaks of his essence or being, his pure existence or his eternal presence, where future and past are enfolded into God's eternal present: *I am*.[5] Existence resides at the heart of God's "godness."[6] He is.

This essentialist reading of God's nature has come under critical scrutiny in twentieth-century theology. It is beyond our purview here to chase this rabbit far. Put simply, essentialist categories for answering the "Who is God?" question have made room for narrative approaches where God's identity and relationship to his creation are more closely linked with the divine economy itself: a bottom-up approach, if you will.[7] The lines dividing God's eternal self (immanence) from his creative/redemptive revelation of himself in time (economic) blur in this narratival move. But not

5. Moses Maimonides, *The Guide of the Perplexed*, trans. S. Pines (Chicago: University of Chicago Press, 1963), 1:61.

6. In classical trinitarian terms, God's essence and his existence are coterminous. For creaturely realities where the two are distinguished, existence occurs because of an external cause. Such cannot be the case with God because no external agent brings about his existence. See Thomas Aquinas, *Summa Theologiae* 1.3.4.

7. For a first-rate example of narratival approaches to divine identity, see Richard Bauckham, *Jesus and the God of Israel: "God Crucified" and Other Studies on the New Testament's Christology of Divine Identity* (Grand Rapids: Eerdmans, 2008). Bauckham does not deny that biblical and later Jewish writers had an interest in questions about divine nature (essentialist concerns). Nevertheless, their primary "conceptual framework" in understanding God had to do with "divine identity," an identity revealed in the narrated movements of Scripture's witness to the divine economy (6–11).

all are persuaded by the recent trends. The title of one monograph makes the point sharply: *God Is Not a Story.*[8]

A close reading of Exod. 3 within the larger frame of Exodus's name theology may help chart a course between these alternatives. Or put more precisely, Exod. 3 may bring essentialist and narratival concerns into a reciprocal relationship. God's relating to his creatures in acts of creation, revelation, and redemption—the stuff of God's economy—flows from the essential character of God's being. In Aquinas's frame of understanding, the eternal processions of God (immanence) are revealed, even if analogically, in the temporal mission (economy) of God. These two facets remain distinct for an important theological reason: the maintaining of the Creator/creature distinction. Yet they remain distinct in an insoluble and reciprocating relation, the one to the other. Gilles Emery clarifies, "In the mission or temporal processions, explains Saint Thomas, the divine person who is sent forth impresses on the soul of the saints a likeness of his eternal property."[9]

The fine-tuning of these theological categories should be left to those whose pay grade matches the subject matter.[10] Nevertheless, these categories emerging from speculative theology or Christian dogmatics provide helpful, even necessary, hermeneutical keys.

8. Francesca A. Murphy, *God Is Not a Story: Realism Revisited* (Oxford: Oxford University Press, 2007).

9. Gilles Emery, "Trinity and Creation," in *The Theology of Thomas Aquinas*, ed. R. Van Nieuwenhove and J. Wawrykow (Notre Dame: University of Notre Dame Press, 2005), 68. Emery also states, "The procession of the Word and that of the Spirit are not only the source of creation; they extend their influence to the entire divine economy" (67).

10. The secondary literature on this subject is voluminous. Readers may find helpful the essays in *Trinity and Election in Contemporary Theology*, ed. M. T. Dempsey (Grand Rapids: Eerdmans, 2011). Especially instructive is the interlocution between Matthew Levering and Bruce McCormack in their respective readings on Aquinas and the relation between the processions and missions of the Trinity. Matthew Levering, "Christ, the Trinity, and Predestination: McCormack and Aquinas," in Dempsey, *Trinity and Election*, 244–76; Bruce L. McCormack, "Processions and Missions: A Point of Convergence between Thomas Aquinas and Karl Barth," in *Thomas Aquinas and Karl Barth: An Unofficial Catholic-Protestant Dialogue*, ed. B. L. McCormack and T. J. White (Grand Rapids: Eerdmans, 2013), 99–126.

Within Exodus's theological movement as a book, God's revelation of his name emerges from the complex dynamic of his
will to redeem his people. God's revealed self takes a particular
clarifying turn in Exodus as his eternal identity is enmeshed with
his redemptive, covenantal relation with his people.

At the wrestling match on the banks of the Jabbok River, a
narrative I will look at closely in due course, Jacob asks for the
name of his supernatural opponent (Gen. 32). The response is
sharp: "What is that to you?" Admittedly, the episode is strange
on multiple fronts. But the unfolding of the divine name within
the Pentateuch is specifically linked to the exodus event. While the
Jabbok narrative may have a complex religiohistorical backstory
regarding some of its enigmatic elements, its Pentateuchal context
provides a theological significance to the divine reticence. The connotative significance of the name Yhwh is linked with the exodus
episode, and Jacob is not privy to such knowledge yet.

In a similar vein to the Jacob narrative at Jabbok is Exod. 6:2–3,
a text that is central to the name theology of the book of Exodus. "God also spoke to Moses and said to him: 'I am the LORD
[*Yhwh*]. I appeared to Abraham, Isaac, and Jacob as God Almighty
[*El Elyon*], but by my name "The LORD" I did not make myself
known to them'" (Exod. 6:2–3 NRSV). This verse persists as a
source critic's darling. The rationale goes something like this: the
patriarchs knew only the name *El* or *Elohim*, with *Yhwh* appearing
later in Israel's religiohistorical development; the Canaanite religious instincts became borrowed capital for Israel's own developing
religion, Yahwism. This particular religiohistorical narrative is told
often enough not to need full repeating here.[11] In the source critic's
account, Abraham had no concept of the name Yhwh.

While elements of this religiohistorical narrative may ring true,
the canonical presentation differs at crucial points. The patriarchal

---

11. See Rainer Albertz, *A History of Israelite Religion in the Old Testament
Period*, vol. 1, *From the Beginnings to the End of the Monarchy*, Old Testament
Library (Louisville: Westminster John Knox, 1994), 27–32.

history is rife with references to Yhwh. One need only recall Abraham's encounter at the oaks of Mamre in Gen. 18 to problematize an account of the divine name as presented in certain quarters of critical theory. According to the canonical presentation, Abraham knew Yhwh. So what is Exod. 6:3 claiming?

The revealing of the divine name in Exod. 3 and 6 locates God's self-determination to reveal himself within the nexus of his redemptive actions. It is not that Abraham did not know the Semitic phonemes of the divine name. Nevertheless, Abraham's position within the divine economy before the exodus event limits his knowledge of the name's soterial significance, especially given this crucial and defining episode in Israel's covenantal history.[12] This particular moment in the divine economy renders the divine name and its significance in a fuller redemptive frame particular to this moment of divine self-unveiling. By way of extension, a similar claim might be made about the last verse of Jesus's high-priestly prayer in John 17: "I made your name known to them, and I will make it known" (v. 26 NRSV).[13] The disciples were not unaware of the divine name. But this singular moment in the divine economy of redemption attaches a significance to the divine name unknown till this moment of self-unveiling.

It comes as little surprise, then, to find discourse pertaining to the divine name toward the end of the Exodus narrative as well

12. Benno Jacob's classic commentary on Exodus claims, "The two periods of history were not distinguished through the knowledge of one or another Name of God, but through two distinct aspects of God revealed in each period." *The Second Book of the Bible: Exodus*, trans. W. Jacob (Hoboken, NJ: Ktav, 1992), 146. Similarly, Francis Turretin asserts, "In this sense, he says that he had not been known to the patriarchs by his name Jehovah (Exod. 6:3), not as to the signifying word (for the contrary is evident from the book of Genesis), but as to the thing signified." *Institutes of Elenctic Theology*, trans. G. M. Giger and ed. J. T. Dennison Jr. (Phillipsburg: P&R, 1992), 1:185. See also Christopher Seitz, "The Call of Moses and the 'Revelation' of the Divine Name: Source-Critical Logic and Its Legacy," in *Theological Exegesis: Essays in Honor of Brevard S. Childs*, ed. C. Seitz and K. Greene-McCreight (Grand Rapids: Eerdmans, 1999), 145–61.

13. The NIV unfortunately leaves ὄνομος (name) untranslated in its rendering of the text's dynamic sense.

(Exod. 32–34). The golden-calf episode marks another crucial turning point in the divine economy. The either/or character of the Decalogue and God's covenantal claims on Israel are now tested: "I am your God, and you will be my people" (cf. Exod. 6:7). Israel's worship of the golden calf breaks the covenantal claim "You shall have no other gods before me" (20:3). When God interrupts his conversation with Moses while Moses is on Sinai's heights, the reader of Exodus realizes that the stakes are high. God makes use of the cold and distant second-person possessive pronoun and tells Moses to go to "*your* people" (32:7, 11–12) because they have offended against "my law" (cf. 32:8). The either/or moment arrives. Yet Moses intercedes. God in his mercy relents. Immediately following God's relenting, Moses asks the unthinkable: he wants to see the glory of God. Then in theophanic glory Yhwh passes by (33:12–23) and in the next chapter (34:6–7) gives a detailed exposition of the significance of his own name. "And he passed in front of Moses, proclaiming, 'Yhwh, Yhwh'" (34:6, cf. NIV).

Yhwh's proclamation of his own name *is* the revelation of his glory. The thirteen *middot* (attributes) of God listed by Yhwh himself (34:6–7) reveal the character of the divine name and in so doing reveal the character of Yhwh.[14] He is merciful and severe. The name of Yhwh entails existence and being but does so in a redemptive and revelatory context where his being is made available by his own unveiling. Moreover, this self-unveiling locates God's being as merciful and severe, the two necessarily conjoined, with God's mercy shaping our understanding of his severity, and his severity as an exercise of his holiness, wisdom, and justice. By way of extension, the intertextual appeal to Exod. 34:6–7 that runs throughout the Minor Prophets reveals Israel's continual struggle to come to terms with Yhwh's mercy and severity. Like Jacob at the River Jabbok, Israel's covenantal existence endures as a

---

14. Jewish tradition lists thirteen aspects (*middot*) of God's mercy said to be revealed in Exod. 34:6–7.

wrangling with its merciful and severe God, even till the break of day (Hosea 12:1–6).

The revealing of the divine name and the redemptive context of this self-unveiling are of some consequence when coming to terms with the Trinity and the Old Testament. Yhwh's mission to create and redeem does not exhaust the scope of God's being. As various episodes within the Old Testament attest, the being of God resists domestication of any sort. Moses's fearful encounter with Yhwh in Exod. 4:24–26 is case in point. Nevertheless, God's revealed being remains ensconced within a salvific context where his mercy and severity come to the fore.[15] As mentioned above, the missions of God in time (creation and redemption) reveal the eternal processions of God in God's subsisting relations. The two remain distinct yet inseparable.

Yhwh: The One and the Many

A peculiar facet of the identity of Yhwh, merciful and severe, emerges in the Old Testament's textual witness. In certain streams of tradition, Yhwh has the ability to differentiate himself from himself without fragmenting his deity or divine being. Benjamin Sommer identifies this feature of Yhwh as "the divine fluidity model."[16] For example, Yhwh's location at Teman or Hebron may

15. Richard Muller recounts Calvin's comments on Ps. 8, in which he prioritizes the relational/revelational character of the divine name over subtle speculations regarding God's essence. For Calvin, God is known primarily by his works: "It [God's name] ought rather to be referred to the works and properties by which he is known than to his essence." Calvin's prioritization of the relational/revelational emerges from a Reformed emphasis on the applicability of doctrine and exegesis. Calvin is happy enough to affirm, for example, the traditional metaphysical understanding of the inseparability of God's essence and his existence. But he does so when such claims flow organically from the exegesis of Scripture itself, i.e., Calvin's comments on the name "Jehovah" in Ps. 83:18 (Eng. verse numbering). *Post-Reformation Reformed Dogmatics: The Rise and Development of Reformed Orthodoxy, ca. 1520 to ca. 1725*, vol. 3, *The Divine Essence and Attributes* (Grand Rapids: Baker Academic, 2003), 251.

16. Benjamin Sommer, *The Bodies of God and the World of Ancient Israel* (Cambridge: Cambridge University Press, 2009), 38.

be particular to that place so that Yhwh's presence there differs somewhat from Yhwh at Jerusalem. Absalom's trek back to Hebron to make vows to Yhwh there when Jerusalem was just around the corner may make some sense of this religious dynamic (2 Sam. 15:7).[17] The evidence in the Old Testament for the distinction between Yhwh's self at various locations is scant. Therefore, building theological or metaphysical conclusions on this basis remains thin. The relationship between Yhwh and his *mal'akh* (messenger/angel), however, is another matter.

The relationship between Yhwh and the angel of Yhwh is of material consequence when attending to the trinitarian character of the Old Testament. In some instances, the angel of Yhwh resists any identification with Yhwh's being (cf. 2 Sam. 24:16–18). In these cases, the angel of Yhwh exists as a messenger or herald sent at Yhwh's behest to do his bidding. In other instances, however, differentiating between Yhwh and his *mal'akh* becomes more problematic and, one should add, more interesting.

As Gerhard von Rad claims, "The most interesting are those which are not really able to distinguish between Jahweh and his angel, and which therefore do not take the angel as only a messenger, but as a form of manifestation of Jahweh himself. The angel of Jahweh is Jahweh himself, appearing to human beings in human form."[18] In line with Sommer's "divine fluidity model," certain traditions within the Old Testament narrate the *mal'akh's* identity in such a way that differentiating him from Yhwh becomes difficult if not impossible. Herman Bavinck states, "So much is clear: that in the *Mal'akh Yahweh*, who is preeminently worthy of that name, God (esp. his Word) is present in a very special sense. This is very evident from the fact that though distinct from Jehovah, this Angel of Jehovah bears the same name, has the same power, effects the same deliverance, dispenses the same blessings,

17. Sommer, *Bodies of God*, 39.
18. Gerhard von Rad, *Old Testament Theology*, trans. by D. M. G. Stalker (New York: Harper & Row, 1962), 1:287.

and is the object of the same adoration."[19] The plurality of persons within a unified divine essence remains an Old Testament problem, leaning against the notion that such trinitarian logic is foisted onto the text rather than drawn from it.

The texts supporting the plurality of persons within a unity of divine being are the usual suspects. Rublev's notable *Icon of the Trinity* depicts Abraham's encounter with Yhwh in Gen. 18. In the narrative movement of this text, the three visitors become a single persona as one figure, Yhwh embodied, emerges and speaks directly with Abraham. Later in the Abrahamic narratives, the angel of Yhwh halts the sacrificial knife and commences to speak to Abraham in Yhwh's first-person voice (Gen. 22:16). A similar dynamic between the *mal'akh* and Yhwh occurs in the calling of Gideon (Judg. 6:17–40). The blessing of Jacob in Gen. 48:15–16 links together *mal'akh* and *Elohim* in synonymous parallelism.

Along this line of inquiry, one fascinating text emerges as central to the discussion at hand because of its own reception in the compositional history of the Old Testament itself: Jacob's wrestling match with a "man" (אִישׁ) in Gen. 32:22–32. The wrestling match at the River Jabbok continues to bewilder and capture the imagination of readers because the text is fraught with enigmatic elements. Jacob sends his family and servants across the southern banks of the river to its northern side. "And Jacob was left alone." Why? One practical reason is the thwarting effect such a herd of folks may have had on Esau's violent anger. From a narrative standpoint, Jacob's remaining behind and alone provides the opportunity for this providential sparring match with "a man."[20] Von Rad makes much of the mental strain and focus Jacob suffers because of his unavoidable future engagement with Esau.[21] And yet

19. Herman Bavinck, *The Doctrine of God*, trans. W. Hendriksen (Edinburgh: Banner of Truth, 1997), 257.

20. Luther understands Jacob's desire to be alone as indicative of his pressing need to pray.

21. Gerhard von Rad, *Genesis: A Commentary*, Old Testament Library (Philadelphia: Westminster, 1972), 320.

out of nowhere, on the riverbanks of the Jabbok, a man appears, and this event is far more dangerous than any encounter with Esau.

The two men begin to wrestle. Again, we are left in enigmatic territory. Why did they begin to wrestle? We are not told. Nevertheless, Jacob (*ya'aqob*) wrestles (*ye'abeq*) with a man by the river Jabbok (*ya'bboq*) until the break of dawn. The assonance of the Hebrew words has the poetic effect of emphasizing the centrality of this episode as it pertains to Jacob's name and its alteration. For Jacob, the defining moment of his life is going to happen the next day, when he meets Esau. For Yhwh, however, the defining moment of Jacob's life is this encounter by the Jabbok. Here Jacob strives with God, prevails/perseveres, and receives a blessing, forever altering his identity and his gait. No longer is he "Heel-grabber" (Gen. 25:26, my trans.). Now he is Israel, one who has "striven with God" (32:28). He has a limp for the rest of his life to prove it.

The details of this text necessitate critical and creative inquiry. For example, how can Jacob strive with God and prevail? For obvious theological reasons certain Jewish interpreters identify this man as the protective angel of Esau. Prevailing over God is inconceivable and theologically offensive. Other interpretive questions emerge. Why does "the man" need to depart before the breaking of dawn? Why does the man refuse to give his name? Interpretive questions such as these persist as the material of scholarly discussion and disagreement. Pursuing their answers would remove us from our particular inquiry, yet admittedly, the text is riddled with enigmatic elements. Despite these uncertainties, the interpretive framework provided by Hosea 12:4–6 is of some consequence for our trinitarian investigation.

Hosea 12:4 (12:5 MT) identifies "the man" with whom Jacob wrestles as a *mal'akh*. This identification comes as no surprise because it is not out of the ordinary for an angel to be referred to by the term אִישׁ (man).[22] The "confusion" arises in verse 5 (v. 6

22. Sommer, *Bodies of God*, 41.

MT), where the prophet also identifies the figure as Yhwh. As Sommer clarifies, "The reason for the apparent confusion between God and angel in these verses from Hosea is simply that both passages, Hosea 12 and Genesis 32, reflect a belief that the selves of an angel and the God Yhwh could overlap or that a small-scale fragment of Yhwh can be termed a *mal'akh*."[23] The Hosea text understands the figure of Gen. 32 as both an angel and Yhwh, equally and at the same time.[24]

Perhaps Hosea's interpretation of Jacob at Jabbok hovers in the material world of speculative Christian theology, with its distinction between *person* and *essence*. I am not claiming that Hosea was thinking in these terms. Therefore I am not basing the argument on human, authorial intentionality. Nevertheless, ontology and epistemology—the being of God and our understanding of God's being—are related but distinct matters. One shouldn't expect Hosea, Moses, or David, for example, to be conceptually aware of the full ontological implications of their prophetic words regarding the divine being.

Put positively, the ontological dimension of Scripture's witness allows the *signa* (verbal sign) to be fitted properly to Scripture's *res significata* (subject matter of the verbal sign), a subject matter made available by the full and total witness of a two-Testament canon. Moreover, the distinctions made within the speculative theological traditions of the church are made for the sake of coming to terms with the claims of Scripture's total witness, a point that Lewis Ayres and others have made persuasively.[25] Distinguish-

---

23. Sommer, *Bodies of God*, 41.

24. The incommunicability of the Tetragrammaton (YHWH) to creatures became a matter of some consequence in Protestant orthodoxy's reaction to Socinianism. If the Tetragrammaton is predicated on the *mal'akh* of the Old Testament, then by necessary conclusion the angel must be an uncreated angel and not a created one, a "prelude to [Christ's] incarnation." Turretin, *Institutes*, 1:185. See also, Muller, *Post-Reformation Reformed Dogmatics*, 3:259–60, 264.

25. Lewis Ayres, *Nicaea and Its Legacy: An Approach to Fourth-Century Trinitarian Theology* (Oxford: Oxford University Press, 2004), 31–40; see also David Yeago, "The New Testament and Nicene Dogma: A Contribution to the Recovery of Theological Exegesis," *Pro Ecclesia* 3 (1994): 152–64.

ing between *person* and *essence* remains at the heart of trinitarian theology and biblical interpretation.

The relation between Yhwh and his *mal'akh*—and by extension his Spirit and Word/Wisdom—indicates an overlap of identities and a distinction between persons at the same time.[26] This particular biblical description reinforces Aquinas's identification of Yhwh with the divine essence or being rather than with a particular *hypostasis* or *persona* of the Godhead: thus Yhwh is not identified as the Father *simpliciter* (without complication).[27]

Richard Muller helpfully describes the orthodox Protestant view: "Given, moreover, that the name 'Jehovah' belongs to God *essentialiter*, *absoluté*, and *indisctincté* apart from an identification or determination of the persons of the Godhead, Scripture can also apply the name and the texts in which it occurs to individual persons, namely, to Christ. The threefold glory of Isaiah 6:3 is, thus, applied to Christ by the evangelist John."[28] Yhwh as God's personal name refers to the divine Godhead in its fullness, the divine essence equally shared by the three persons. As such, Yhwh can be predicated on any of the divine persons without remainder. And at the same time, the name Yhwh is not the sole possession/indicator of any one particular person. Yhwh *is* the Father, Son, and Holy Spirit in their coequal sharing of the divine essence in its fullness.[29]

26. Well worth pursuing is Yhwh's special provenance as it pertains to creation and redemption as well as the "fittingness" of the Word and the Spirit as agents of Yhwh's single will to create and redeem. I thank my colleague Carl Beckwith for making this point clear. See also Boris Bobrinskoy, *The Mystery of the Trinity: Trinitarian Experience and Vision in the Biblical and Patristic Tradition*, trans. A. P. Gythiel (Crestwood, NY: Saint Vladimir's Seminary Press, 1999), 31–49.

27. Aquinas, *Summa Theologiae* 1.13.11.

28. Richard Muller, *Post-Reformation Reformed Dogmatics: The Rise and Development of Reformed Orthodoxy, ca. 1520 to ca. 1725*, vol. 4, *The Triunity of God* (Grand Rapids: Baker Academic, 2003), 303.

29. The danger of identifying Yhwh as the divine essence is the introduction of a fourth member into the Trinity, to wit, the essence as an independent transcendent agent. Paul R. Hinlicky identifies this danger and rightly steers clear of it when he claims, "I would argue that there is no divine essence existing apart transcendentally causing things in general, which may or may not be connected to its own real presence

Conclusion

The rise of historical consciousness in modernity brought with it many positive results for engaging the biblical material. Such a claim resists easy disputation. On the other hand, the reducing of the biblical material to its historical/literary origin—original author, original audience, immediate circumstances giving rise to the subject under discussion, and/or the complex tradition-building process leading to the text's final form—risks cutting Scripture from its ontological subject matter. The hermeneutical backbone of modern criticism, in the oft-repeated phrase of Brevard Childs, altered Scripture's status from a witness to divine revelation into a source for critical reconstruction—literary, historical, or otherwise. Once the historical excavation of the text ends, whether in reconstruction of the historical or literary-critical background, attendance to the text's literal sense concludes as well. The Christian interpreter must strain to affirm the trinitarian character of the Old Testament with these governing hermeneutical instincts deployed. Yhwh's triune identity, on this account, is a homiletical extra, not a close reading of the text itself.

The church's interpretive tradition, on the other hand, keeps the verbal character of Scripture and its divine subject matter insolubly linked when attending to the Scripture's literal sense. To affirm the Old Testament's trinitarian character or to identify Yhwh as the Father, Son, and Holy Spirit are attempts at allowing the Old Testament's own idiom to have a constraining role in the characterization of God as one in essence and three in person. The language of Nicaea would be foreign to the intellectual horizons of Moses or Isaiah. Such formulations are waiting in time for

---

in the Son and blessing in the Spirit as the eternal Father. If that is so, the divine essence *is* the Father of the Son and breather of the Spirit." To speak of Yhwh as the divine essence *is* to speak of the divine essence as Father, Son, and Holy Spirit in their eternal processions. "Quaternity or Patrology," *Pro Ecclesia* 23 (2014): 52. Aquinas's understanding of the persons of the Trinity as "subsisting relations" avoids the danger of isolating the divine essence from the personal relations in their distinction. Relation in God *is* the divine essence. *Summa Theologiae* 1.29.4.

reflection and clarification. But what must be maintained is that the formulations of Nicaea are exegetically grounded attempts to provide a theological and hermeneutical framework for Scripture's own total witness regarding the identity of the one God with whom we have to do.

The distinction between essence and person arises in speculative theology for the sake of allowing Scripture's total witness regarding the divine being to have its say.[30] Hermeneutical assumptions governed by the anteriority of faith's confession and commitments are present from beginning to end. Such a claim need not be denied in a feigned attempt at hermeneutical neutrality. At the same time, the verbal character of the Old Testament is itself fertile soil for a trinitarian hermeneutic where the unity of the divine essence and diversity of the divine personae are affirmed, as Gen. 32:22–32 and Hosea 12:1–6 attest. In fact, the Old Testament's own self-presentation regarding Yhwh's singularity and diversity of personae constrains the faithful reader toward this interpretive conclusion.

---

30. See Gilles Emery, "Essentialism or Personalism in the Treatise on God in St. Thomas Aquinas?," in *Trinity in Aquinas* (Ann Arbor, MI: Sapientia, 2003), 165–208.

EPILOGUE

It's easy enough to sit in an ivory academic tower and pontificate on what "the Church" should be doing. I live in that rarified world where exegetical detail and theological pursuits define the joys and priorities of the community: a divinity school. I warn my students against a seminarian's ego and the dangers of abusing knowledge as a pastoral will to power. And I could continue in my efforts to qualify what I'm about to say, disabusing the reader against any hint of arrogant or smug professorial punditry. But I'm going to take a risk and make a claim because I am a parishioner, and I have hopes and dreams for my students. So here goes: *The church's long-term health and faithful witness rests on its commitment to seeking after God's Word in Holy Scripture.* Of course, other ecclesial matters are important. But a doctrine of Scripture's sufficiency means that the church's access to what gives it life, the person and work of Jesus Christ, is through the front doors of Holy Scripture.

My Protestant blood is on full display here, and I do not wish in any way to diminish the importance of the church's sacramental life. I can't and won't say everything here on the necessary interrelation between Word and Sacrament except for the fact that they are necessarily interrelated! Nevertheless, the temptation for greener pastures other than a passionate and pastoral attendance to Scripture's unique and revered role in Christ's church remains one of the devil's greatest achievements. Amos warns about a famine of God's Word, a famine that makes diminishing food supplies pale in comparison (Amos 8:11). His prophetic warning is a haunting reminder of the church's dependence on God's Word for its very existence.

This book is nowhere near a final word on faithful reading practices. Nothing is said in this book, for example, about the "piety" of Scripture's anticipated readers. Augustine and Calvin would rightly frown on this oversight. Nothing is said about the relation of ethics and liturgy. Isaiah, Hosea, and their entire prophetic cohort would shake their heads. As mentioned in the introduction, this book aims to aid readers of the Bible in their understanding of the material and formal features of the Old Testament in the Christian canon. How does Scripture's literary character relate to Scripture's subject matter, the Triune God? These two canonical features resist dissolution and alter one's approach to biblical exegesis. Therefore the modest scope of this book is offered in hope—hope that Christian readers, lay and ordained, will place their confidence and joy in the promises that God attaches to his Word.

I've tried to avoid too heavy a hand in providing a "method" that easily follows a "Do this first and now this second" approach. Rather, this book aims to give students a set of instincts and expectations that will be refined by an ongoing attendance to the task itself: reading Scripture's material form in light of its theological subject matter. The story of Karl Barth's parting words to his students at Bonn is often repeated: "Exegesis, exegesis and yet more exegesis! Keep to the Word, to the scripture that has been given us."[1] I think about Barth's parting words in view of my own students because, as mentioned above, I know that the tasks

---

1. Eberhard Busch, *Karl Barth: His Life from Letters and Autobiographical Texts*, trans. J. Bowden (Grand Rapids: Eerdmans, 1976), 259.

of pastoral life range far beyond coffee, the study, and an open Bible. I have friends in pastoral ministry who warn me against such idealized and idyllic expectations. Still, it is the open Bible that sustains and energizes every component of pastoral ministry and, for that matter, Christian existence. People need Jesus. And Jesus Christ stands at the door of his own Word and knocks.

SCRIPTURE INDEX

SUBJECT INDEX

121